Price _____   **12.00**   1405

Title _____

Condition - LN VG G (AC) Location HGN-L

[ ] _____ Bent

↳ BOARD EDGE _____ Bumped

[ ] _____ Creasing to Cover ↳ SOME Edge Wear

↳ SOME _____ Shelf Wear [ ] _____ Sunned

[ ] Spine Creased [ ] Remainder Mark

[ ] _____ Foxing

[ ] _____ Soiling

[ ] No Marks in Text [ ] _____ Underlining

[ ] Pages Yellowed [ ] _____ Highlighting

[ ] Weak Hinge(s) [ ] _____ Marginal Marks

[ ] _____ Tear(s) to DJ [ ] _____ Shelf Wear to DJ

Notes SOME MOISTURE RIPPLING OF
PGS. FROM HUMIDITY
    SOME ODOR

*This sticker is removable.

B00BHC96B0

COLLECTOR'S

PROGRESS

BY

WILMARTH LEWIS

NEW YORK ALFRED A. KNOPF

MCMLI

COLLECTOR'S PROGRESS

TO

EDWARD CLARK STREETER, M.D.

1874–1947

COLLECTOR, TEACHER, FRIEND

ACKNOWLEDGMENT

I WISH *to express my thanks to the* Atlantic Monthly *for permission to reprint about a third of this book which was originally published in that magazine. It should be added that although the material is the same, the form in which it is now written is quite different. When Mr. Knopf persuaded me to tell the story of the Walpole collection at Farmington, it became necessary to write several new chapters and to rewrite those that had appeared in the* Atlantic. *I am also indebted to the editors of the* New Colophon *for permission to print a page that, in substance, first appeared in one of its numbers.*

Sections of the book have been read (and improved) by Messrs. John Carter, George T. Goodspeed, Lewis Hanke, Dudley Massey, Keyes D. Metcalf, Thomas W. Streeter, Chauncey Brewster Tinker, Lawrence C. Wroth, Father J. Leonard, and the late Lathrop Harper; all of the book has been read by Messrs. R. W. Chapman, Allen T. Hazen, and R. W. Ketton-Cremer, who made many suggestions that I have followed. The editor of the Atlantic, *Mr. Edward Weeks, not only was encouraging, but specifically improved sev-*

eral passages. I am aware that the publishing world declines to accept credit for the immense help that it gives its authors, but in fairness to him and three others I ought to say that their criticisms have resulted in a much better book. The three to whom I want to express my particular thanks are Messrs. Wilson Follett, John T. Winterich, and Alfred Knopf. This book would have been out long ago but for them—and been much the worse for it.

My secretary, Miss Julia McCarthy, has typed and retyped the entire book a dozen times with inextinguishable patience and has helped me with the index.

As always, my greatest debt of acknowledgment is due my wife, who during the past six years has improved every page while patiently enduring the ups and downs that have attended the book's composition.

Farmington, Connecticut
  January 1951

ILLUSTRATIONS

ALL THE OBJECTS ILLUSTRATED ARE FROM
THE AUTHOR'S COLLECTION.

Lady Walpole are flowers, shells, a pallet and pencils, to mark her love of the arts; their favourite hounds in the foreground and a view of Houghton in the distance. This painting is from the united efforts of Eckardt and Wootton, and is considered a masterpiece of art; the portraits of Sir Robert and Lady Walpole are from the miniatures by Zincke, the hounds and view of Houghton by Wootton. The black and gold frame enclosing the picture, one of the finest specimens of carving, is by Gibbons, displaying with wonderful effect the arms of the family, enriched with Cupid figures as supporters, birds, fruit, grapes and foliage, most beautifully designed and perfect as a work of art."

The picture was bought by the third Marquess of Lansdowne, whose modesty declined a dukedom and the prime ministership, and who was a notable collector. He was a grandson of Walpole's correspondent the Countess of Upper Ossory. The portrait was No. 77 at Lansdowne House, Berkeley Square. It was sold at Christie's, March 7, 1930, lot 40, to Dighton & Co., from whom I bought it.

ILLUSTRATIONS

ILLUSTRATIONS

INTRODUCTION

"It will look, I fear, a little like arrogance in a private man to give a printed description of his villa and collection." This was written in 1784 by Horace Walpole in the Preface to his *Description of Strawberry Hill.* He was speaking for all collectors who write about their houses and collections. The collector is afraid of being thought arrogant if he publishes an account of his collection; but he has a still stronger fear, the fear that the world will not know that he has a collection worth writing about.

Our house was called by *Life* after a "Visit" to it in 1944 "a simple Colonial American home." *Life* was speaking of that part of the house we call "the old house." As far as we can make out, it was built in 1784. Once inside the front door, the visitor finds himself in a hall elaborately paneled and carved in 1784 in white pine. The hall leads to a modern addition. As the visitor goes down six steps and continues along the hall, he passes on either side pictures, water-color drawings, and prints of Horace Walpole's house, Strawberry Hill, at Twickenham, twelve miles from

Hyde Park Corner. At the end of the hall our visitor reaches the "new library," so called to distinguish it from the library in the old part of the house and a still newer library north of the long hall. If the visitor comes into the house by a south door, he goes through a shorter hall that is also lined with pictures and drawings relating to Walpole and Strawberry Hill.

The new library, which was designed by William Adams Delano in 1928, is paneled in butternut. It has light on three sides and a barrel-vaulted ceiling, eighteen and a half feet high. Except for a fireplace and a door opposite it that leads to the garden, bookshelves go around the room to the height of about ten feet; four bays greatly increase the space for books. Above the books are portraits of Walpole's relations. There are about 5,000 books in the room, mainly "background" books for the study of Horace Walpole, whose letters are usually regarded as the best in the language. These background books are the works of eighteenth-century literary figures, with special sections on Boswell, Johnson, Gray, Mason, and Chatterton; a large collection of plays; topography, with particular emphasis on London, Twickenham, Eton, Cambridge, and Norfolk (the places with which Walpole was most concerned) ; the arts; books about Walpole and his family and friends; a French section; sermons; the *Gentleman's Magazine, Annual Regis-*

THE "NEW LIBRARY"

ter, Monthly Review, and other eighteenth-century periodicals and transactions.

The heart of the collection is in the newest library, the one that opens off the long hall. This is a fireproof room. In it are some 3,000 books: all the editions of Walpole's works; the books that he owned; the productions of his private press at Strawberry Hill; and several hundred reference books. In this room are more than 6,000 originals or photostats of the estimated 7,000-odd letters to and from Walpole still in existence and Walpole's other known manuscripts. Also here in filing cases are thousands of index cards relating to these letters and manuscripts, to Walpole's library, to the contents of his house, and to many other eighteenth-century matters, including a detailed case history of Walpole's gout. A "diurnal" records what is known of every day in his life from his twentieth year to his eightieth. All these files and cards are an attempt to adapt American business methods and gadgets to scholarly problems.

Recently two small stack rooms have been added. These more than double the space for files and indexes and provide shelves for 6,000 books, together with about 10,000 eighteenth-century letters other than those to and from Walpole, and the cards that refer to them. On the shelves are several thousand auction and booksellers' catalogues that contain Walpoliana, the *British Museum Catalogue* and other bibliographical works, and Parliamentary reports and journals.

A paragraph should perhaps be given to a section of miscellaneous books in a guest room. This library I call "Lewis's Folly." My intention was, at the outset, to acquire every book printed in Britain between 1751 and 1800 that is not in the Yale Library (of which my collection will one day be a part). No one knows how many books were printed in those fifty years—perhaps there were as many as 300,000—but the plan was not so fantastic as it sounds, for the Yale Library appears to have about eighty per cent of the books already. It would be useful to have one library (even though its buildings are thirty miles apart) where students of the eighteenth century can find all the books of that half century. "Lewis's Folly" has already proved of great help to me and the other editors of *The Yale Edition of Horace Walpole's Correspondence* (a work I began in 1933 and which I hope will be finished—all fifty volumes of it —in 1965), but I have modified the original plan. Although the new stack rooms at Farmington give extra shelves at the moment, and an unused squash court there will one day provide space for 30,000 more volumes, there simply would not be room for all the books still missing. So I have stopped buying books on subjects that are already strongly represented at Yale—Americana, music, medicine (except books on the gout), theology, verse, and fiction. What does this leave? The immense number of little-known books that throw light on the daily lives of eighteenth-century men and women and that are particularly needed for the study of Horace Walpole, the chief social historian of their day.

A good many visitors come to our house in the course of a year. They come from all over the world. Many of them are eighteenth-century experts who want to see whatever I may have that bears upon their specialty. Within the year this has included such diverse subjects as bindings, Wedgwood, coins and medals, sale catalogues, play-bills, Thomas Patch, Joseph Banks, and the Stamp Act. Whatever the subject may be, Walpole probably said something about it, and there may be that there is at Farmington a book, manuscript, picture, print, or curiosity that will throw fresh light upon it. This will lead us on to another book, letter, or what-not, on and on, until we can endure no more.

Whether the visit is of minutes or of days, and whether the visitor is an eighteenth-century expert or not, the same question is invariably asked: "How did you become interested in Horace Walpole?"

COLLECTOR'S PROGRESS

I

I

MY FIRST collection was of houseflies. It was kept in a discarded cigar box that was thrown out one day without my knowledge or consent. A year later, at the age of six, I collected shells at Santa Cruz, California. This collection was also thrown out without my knowledge or consent. It was thus brought home to me early that one must be on one's guard against non-collectors.

Forty-odd years ago all my contemporaries collected something. Most boys went in for cigar bands and election cards. I regarded such collections as trash, and at the age of ten went all out for the ultimate: stamps.

My album is before me, "*The International Postage Stamp Album.* Illustrated with Engravings. 4,000. 1901 Edition. New York. The Scott Stamp & Coin Co., Limited." Its decorated green boards are so worn that the boy on the left, who is innocently holding a banner of Imperial Germany, is all but effaced below the waist, and his companion's banner can only just be identified as Spain's. The album came to me from my much older brothers, who had long since lost interest in it. I printed my name on the inside cover with ornamental flourishes, and below wrote: "1625 Central Ave., Alameda, Cal." On the opposite flyleaf I added: "Mar. 31, '06—Began—300," and the unfolding statistics:

> Jan. 1, '07—1,630
> Collection worth Feb. 1—$180.93
> Feb. 16—2,359
> Mar. 1—2,650
> April 1—2,930

The spectacular development of the first year was partly owing to the abandonment of his collection by an older boy, who gave his book to me. This meant that I had a great many duplicates, and it put me in a position of advantage to barter and sell at Christ Church, which my family attended and where I was employed in the choir. Many of my colleagues were stamp-collectors; those who were not became so.

The choir, except for the rector's long and noisy sermons, was delightful. Dressed in cassock and cotta, you were the center of attention moving solemnly along behind the crucifer, consulting your hymnal briefly from time to time before raising your head in replenished song. You were an initiate in divine mysteries, marked off from the laity by your costume, by your active participation in ancient rites, and by your pronouncing "and" "ond." It was a joy to pass the family pew and meet the family's eyes without acknowledgment, especially just as you were singing "ond." The choir was a man's world, ritualistic, competitive. It was a world in which a business note had been introduced, since we were paid for our services.

As time went on I became the second-highest-paid boy in the choir, receiving fifty cents a month and the distinction of wearing a silver cross. Only one boy was higher paid: he sang all the solos, for which he got seventy-five cents a month and the honor of wearing a gold cross. He was one of the last to become a stamp-collector.

The duplicates of my stamps I tipped into oblong gray-green notebooks; the price of each, according to Scott, was written beneath—or, rather, half Scott's price, since everyone knew that for some reason Scott was inflated. I took my entire stock to church on pay days and for several months managed to collect all the choir money, which in a good month would run as high as three dollars and sixty-five cents.

After pay day I would take my new money across the Bay to San Francisco, out to Van Ness Avenue (it was then after the Fire), to a dealer who should have been the embodiment of God, but who wasn't. He was a large, disagreeable man, and all he ever said was: "Well, how much have you got this time?" Then he would hand me the next stamp in the series known as the Hawaiian Island Provisional Government, 1893. When I protested feebly that, far from being half Scott's price, it was actually in advance of it, the man would reply that Scott didn't know everything and I could take it or leave it. I always took it, and I would peer into the little envelope a dozen times on the trip home.

My connection with philately and the Church came to a sudden and dramatic end. The choirmaster decided that I should have a solo in the *Te Deum,* in which I bore witness that the Cherubim and Seraphim Continually Do Cry. Even the organ was to remain mute during this testimony. My family, whose attendance at church had become spotty of late owing to the new automobile, came again to the family pew, but their nervous and prideful smiles faded when my great moment was reached for I also remained mute, and the seraphic conduct went unrecorded that day in Alameda. Just before church I had read in the *San Francisco Chronicle* about prima donnas in general and Mme Tetrazzini, who was then singing in San Francisco, in particular. Prima donnas, it appeared, did not sing if they didn't feel like it. As a result of my silence I lost my silver cross, and my salary was reduced. Whereupon (the Tetrazzini

6

touch again) I left the choir. There were still four blank spaces in the Provisional Government, 1893, which is proof of my immaturity as a collector, for a seasoned collector will endure any humiliation to attain his ends.

In three years I became a numismatist. My mother and I were at Leamington, in Warwickshire. I was unhappy and homesick for California and far under weight, and I went on a semi-hunger-strike; that is, I became a problem. There was nothing, apparently, for me to do at Leamington except to get on a tram and go to Warwick, four miles away. After several trips to the Castle, the Beauchamp Chapel, and Leicester's Hospital, Warwick began to pall. And then I found an antique shop with a collection of English coins. They were not expensive, but they were beyond my reach. There was a musty and mysterious atmosphere in the shop, the first antique shop I had ever been in, which worked powerfully upon my imagination. Relics of former ages stretched away into the dim and cluttered distance, out of which the proprietor would emerge with a wan face and narrow steel spectacles that might have been taken from the collection of spectacles, snuffboxes, and teaspoons in a glass case opposite the front door. A way to bridge the barrier between me and the coins suggested itself, for in the solution of such problems lies

7

a collector's peculiar skill: my mother was worried by my not eating; I was worried by not being able to buy the coins; so I proposed that I be paid a dollar a week for eating. The proposal was accepted and went into effect with complete success. I bought the coins one by one, time passed quickly and pleasantly as I rode back and forth to Warwick, I put on a little weight, and lived to get back to California.

For my last collection of this period I turned to butterflies, *Lepidoptera*, a scientific interlude. I had a net without gaps or holes, a bottle of cyanide, black pins, glass plates, forceps, a scalpel, and a cabinet. These supplied the delights of the laboratory and gave me a sense of the precise beauties of system, but the great excitement was in the field. After forty years I can still feel my hot anxiety as a "new" butterfly sailed into view, darted off over the warm summer fields, and finally came to rest, opening and closing its wings. This is what collecting is—the all but unbearable excitement when the longed-for quarry appears, the fierce and crafty pursuit, the cyanide bottle, the black pins, the cabinet, and one additional factor, the admiring and (supreme felicity) envious visitors.

2

The first antiquarian bookshop I ever went into was John Howell's in San Francisco, a few years after the Fire. I was taken there by one of my brothers who was greatly impressed by the appearance in Grant Avenue of a shop in which were old books. Mr. Howell opened his safe for us. Books in a safe! Half a dozen years later I bought my first book as a collector.

This transaction took place in the Brick Row Bookshop at New Haven. The Brick Row had been established in the belief that Yale undergraduates should have an opportunity to build up libraries of their own choosing. Its books were mostly inexpensive editions of the English and American classics. There were no textbooks, which have the chill of death upon them. In that shop many undergraduates overcame the awe or dislike that most people have of books. It was one thing to be told in class: "The assignment for next Monday is one hundred and one pages of Hazlitt," and another to find an early edition of Hazlitt for yourself. The assignment was a chore, the discovery a pleasure. We were left alone in the Brick Row and were free to wander about, taking books down from the shelves and putting them back. The books we encountered in the classroom assumed a new meaning with each new guise in which we found them. Even the greatest books, even Shakespeare, gradually became familiar and unpretentious.

Greatly daring, I bought a book, a copy of *Alice in*

Wonderland, under the impression that it was the first edition. When it was subsequently pointed out to me that the title-page bore a New York imprint and the line: "Seventy-seventh thousand," I gave up book-collecting. This disillusionment lasted until I returned to Yale after the war and began, along with half of New Haven, to collect the works of John Masefield.

I had met him when he came to Yale to lecture in 1917, and in the next year when he turned up at Camp Kearney, San Diego, to talk about Anglo-American relations in a Y.M.C.A. hut. (He followed an Australian lady who gave bird calls.) I took him on a sightseeing trip that included the theosophical community at Point Loma, and although we failed to meet the Purple Mother, we did meet the community's poet, who led us about

       with pilgrim steps in amice grey

among the buildings of purple glass, rendering homage to Masefield the while. As we drove away, my guest said in his high little voice, which did not drop at the end of the sentence: "If one had to choose between that sort of thing and the Prussian sort of thing, I think one would choose the Prussian sort of thing." A few weeks later we met again on the pier in New York at the gangplank of the *Aquitania.* The third night out I came down with mumps, but the future Laureate called at my crowded cabin twice a day with books and cheer. Naturally, I collected Masefield when I returned from the war.

Time healed the wound inflicted by my experience with *Alice,* and when I went to England in the summer of 1922, I found it easy and natural to enter whatever bookshop I came across and to spend hours taking books down from the shelves and putting most, but not all, of them back. Such grazing on the common of literature can be more rewarding than an entire English "major." One moves from clump to clump, from Defoe, Gay, and Garth to Gray, Collins, and Cowper, or to a thousand other authors, earlier or later, without plan or direction, according to the arrangement of the shelves. In those shops I first saw, over and over again, the multitude of books that never get into an English "major"—the household books of the last century, the angling and sporting books, the color-plate books, and books of travel. Bookshops ceased being Poets' Corners and booksellers were discovered to be human beings.

At Newbury an American friend had found a shop so filled with treasures that not only his library and mine, but that of two other friends could be made by them. The shop was not, strictly speaking, a bookshop at all. It was a draper's shop, presided over by the widow of the man who had collected the books.

We gathered that although the books might have formed the stock of a small provincial bookseller, the deceased booklover had not had the heart to part with them.

The four of us started up the narrow stairs. On the landing I picked off the shelves what I took to be a first edition of *Maud*. Beside it was a first edition of the *Idylls of the King*. The other three made equally sensational discoveries. Sindbad in the cave of diamonds was not more dazzled. A large room was crowded with books from floor to ceiling. We had to step carefully between the books on the floor. Each of us took a quarter of the room as his particular claim. As time went on we specialized; one took nineteenth-century poetry, another nineteenth-century fiction; I appropriated the eighteenth century. We generously gave up nuggets from our claims that "belonged" to another. This went on for nearly four hours, and we got very, very dirty.

On the following day we came again. There were four things we learned to look for: the author, the title, the date, and the bookplate or autographs of former owners. Our knowledge of dates was sketchy; our knowledge of bibliography was even less—we had not yet heard the word. In my pile I had not hesitated to include a set of Fielding, three volumes of which were missing. The summer sun filtered through the windows of the attic; motes rose in the shafts of light, dust from the great books that were passing into our possession.

When we finally came to leave, we had to face the delicate question of price. We had broached it tentatively to our hostess once or twice, but she urged us to go ahead and take what we wanted, it would be time enough to talk about the price later on. After we had washed the grime off under a cold tap for the last time, she asked if eightpence a volume would be satisfactory. I bought two hundred and fifty volumes for the equivalent of about forty dollars. We all had twinges of conscience, but what collector can resist a bargain? Arrangements to ship the books to America were made with surprising ease, and we went away filled with the new importance that our libraries gave us.

Before that summer was out I began to suspect that we had paid just about what the books were worth, but even now, after more than thirty years of book-collecting, I still regard those intoxicating hours at Newbury as one of the great moments of my collecting life. The discovery of old editions of English authors, our luck in getting to them ahead of the great dealers of New York and London, the bloom of enthusiasm unbrushed by reality, all this still hangs about my copies of Bruce's *Travels* and the fourth edition of *Robinson Crusoe*—which alone remain of my great Newbury find.

3

The following summer, in 1923, I went to England again to buy books. I had succumbed, like many amateurs in the twenties, to the fancied delights of having a share in a bookshop. Buying books was great fun; why not buy to sell and make money out of them so that I would have more money to spend on books for my own library? I was luckier than most because I got my money back.

At Plymouth I was met by three friends. We went on a motor-golfing trip through the west of England. At Bath I made the acquaintance of Mr. George Bayntun. Although he fitted into the old-time bookseller pattern in some respects, the scale of his business put him in another category. He was a binder of "standard works," which he turned out at a prodigious rate for the trade. His stand was Lamb's: "To be strong-backed and neat-bound is the desideratum of a volume. Magnificence comes after." Mr. Bayntun was content with a ten-per-cent profit and a turnover so rapid that the great authors of the literature galloped through his shop. Shakespeare, Milton, Sterne, and Thackeray were on an assembly line that moved without a hitch from the country auctions and stately mansions of England to the big bookstores of America. Mr. Bayntun would make up a set of anything you wanted on demand, using the full calf or morocco he had salvaged from books in poor condition. If you wanted a personal touch in your new set, he would paste into it armorial bookplates removed from still other volumes. He sold sets of Smollett and Dickens as other tradesmen sold haddock or peas, but only after he had made certain that each book was up to the standard of craftsmanship that had carried his name around the earth. The books he loved were color-plate books, the Ackermann histories of Oxford and Cambridge and the Colleges, the *Microcosm of London,* Pyne's *Royal Residences,* Nattes's *Bath,* and Repton. He kept them on hand, together with *The Punishments of China* and the *Costumes of Russia* and *Hindoostan.*

Mr. Bayntun was a spare man, older than he looked, with thin sandy hair. He wore a smock in the shop, and after selling a certain number of books he took snuff. The sneeze released fresh energies that were not required to send me on to renewed extravagance. In a few years I was to hear him spoken of with dispraise by bibliographers and bibliophiles as a destroyer of original boards and a perverter of history, but he was too good a business man to destroy the valuable. He was a popularizer with a large and appreciative audience. I still have many of the books I bought from him, including a Repton, uncut and in the original boards, in a box of his manufacture. After twenty-seven years his books are "sound," and with any kind of care they will remain so forever. From one end of this country to the other will be found sets of Gibbon and Johnson in the plain, workmanlike, dress that marks Bayntun's work. He realized that his books were more often than not merely part of the furniture of a house, but he was not a cynical man; the *Rambler* was "not everybody's cup of tea." Those over whom he shook his head were people who failed to glow when shown *The Punishments of China*; he shook his head and, after taking snuff, perhaps asked: "Well, then, sir, what *are* you interested in?"

My motor trip that summer ended at Leamington. My friends were leaving shortly for Paris. "Why go to the Midlands, for God's sake, when you can go to Paris?" they asked. It was not an easy question to answer.

At Leeds I was overtaken by the August bank holiday. Everything was closed for days. I sat in a suicidal frame of mind behind the lace curtains and aspidistras in the lounge of the Station Hotel reading old numbers of the *Bystander* and *Sketch*. On the Tuesday I went on to York and the shop of Mr. Godfrey, close to the Minster. Mr. Godfrey, the most avuncular of old-time booksellers, told me what I should buy. In the evening he took me for a walk on the city walls to cool and comfort me after the day's excitement and to strengthen me for a night in a place that was called "an hotel." (There was a convention meeting in York and all the hotels were full.) The place where I ended up was certainly sinister, but except for one bloodcurdling scream during the night I was not disturbed.

Among the books Mr. Godfrey sold me the next morning was John Heneage Jesse's *George Selwyn and His Contemporaries* (4 vols., 1843), a series of letters addressed to Selwyn "by persons who, in their day moved in the first ranks of wit, genius, and fashion." On a flyleaf of the first volume was written, "With Manuscript Notes by Lady Louisa Stuart," and in a pocket attached to the front cover were Lady Louisa's notes, covering thirty-four octavo pages in her firm, small hand. Each volume bore the bookplate of The Hirsel, a place that meant no more to me than did George Selwyn or Lady Louisa herself. This was a work, said Mr. Godfrey, that should be in every gentleman's library, and on his say-so I bought it, for thirty-five shillings.

At home in Farmington that fall I sat one night waiting for three dinner guests. In front of me were the hundreds of books I had bought during the past two years. They were for the most part inexpensive editions of the English classics, together with my Masefield collection, which I had completed in England with the purchase, long desired, of *Salt-Water Ballads,* 1902. A completed collection is a journey ended, and although I had heard of Masefield manuscripts and corrected proof sheets, which revealed new heights of collecting, the light was fading from my Masefield shelf. "Here," I thought, "is all English literature spread out before me and I am not *really* interested in any of it. Now, if I could only get going on someone—" and there drifted across my mind "outstanding collection," "delightful life."

At this time I was nearing my twenty-eighth birthday and had about five thousand dollars a year to spend on books if I wanted to do so. A year before Alfred Knopf had published a novel of mine, a modest work that *The New Yorker* was to describe twenty-seven years later as a *succès d'estime.* I was a bachelor, living in the village that Henry James had approached across the valley with "a positively thrilled attention," keeping house with the assistance of a Negro couple, Adam and Martha, whose lives were dedicated to the production of good food and the ministration of comfort. I was completely my own master and a born collector. The past two summers

I have missed the page, but in a note, Mr Jesse
says that Lord Corke's marriage with the daugh
ter of — Courtenay, by Lord Sandwich's sister
was dissolved by act of Parl! — It is not true —
They had been long separated and were at daggers-
drawing: but when Lord Corke sued for a divorce
accusing her of intriguing with a low musician,
he could make nothing of it, bring no proof, and
I believe it never came to a trial. She & her friends
declared it a plot against her, framed to effect his
union with Miss Monckton. Miss Monckton & her friends were
not backward in retaliating, so the war of tongues raged
most fiercely. We visited Lady Corke as a (Montagu) cousin
she was a strange looking woman, seeming to me half mad;
some said driven so by persecution. However, shortly
she died, and more shortly Lord Corke married
Miss Monckton; whom the world has only just
been unfortunate enough to lose.

page 318 &c

After marrying her footman, an Irish lad, Lady Harriet
dropped her title and, as Mrs Sturgeon, went over with him
to visit his parents in Ireland. Then she carried him to France
where she put him into the hands of the best masters and
spared no pains to teach him the manners and
behaviour of a gentleman. The soil was good and as yet
unbroken, so she succeeded; for Mr Weddell (Lady Rockingham's
half sister) who knew him in later days, said he was
not ~~any~~ to be distinguished from other men in
good society, except by more exact good breeding

A PAGE FROM LADY LOUISA STUART

of collecting had reduced still lower my enthusiasm
for my second novel, which I conscientiously pecked
away at. In short, as I sat there looking at my books
I was at a climacteric moment when the slightest push
would make me a serious collector.

After dinner on this fateful night my guests asked
to see the books that I had bought during the summer, before we settled down to the business of the
evening, bridge. I gave the first volume of Jesse's
Selwyn to one of them and took out for her Lady
Louisa's notes from their envelope. Presently my
guest insisted on reading them aloud:

"The Coventry children—Lady Maria *was* 'marked
for life,' and, I think, the ugliest *young* woman I ever
beheld. Lady Anne had not the same strong appearance of disease but was scarcely pretty, nor would
have been held at all so, if—if—one must speak out
—if a modest woman, a part she disdained playing
from her first beginning. Both sisters married, and
both were divorced."

"Poor Miss Pelham had always been fond of play,
at which the impatience of her disposition made her
always sure to lose. As she grew old, all other passions
merged in that of gaming, carried to a height equal
to what it ever was in any man. She ruined herself
and would have ruined her sister, if the mild and excellent Miss Mary's friends had not risen in a body,

and almost forced the latter to leave the house where they lived together, and withdraw to one of her own: which the other never forgave. Poor, poor, Miss Pelham! She was a person one could not help pitying with all her faults. I have myself seen her at that villainous faro-table, putting the guinea she had perhaps borrowed on a card—with the tears running down her face—the wreck of what had been high-minded and generous."

"Mr. Fox. Lord Holland's education of him will account for many of his faults, but also for some of his virtues. It was a system of the most unlimited indulgence of every passion, whim, and caprice. A great dinner was given at Holland House to all the foreign ministers. The children came in at the dessert; Charles, then in petticoats, spying a large bowl of cream in the middle of the table, had a desire to get into it. Lord Holland insisted he should be gratified and in spite of Lady Holland's remonstrances, had it placed on the floor for the child to jump in and splash about at his pleasure."

That night we played no bridge. Lady Louisa had for us a special fascination, for she might have been a neighbor of mine, a relative of my guests, a lady who in her day had also "moved in the first ranks of wit, genius, and fashion."

When my guests left I went to my small collection

of books on eighteenth-century life to find out about this Lady Louisa Stuart who had come in answer to my wish for a person to collect. And then occurred one of those coincidences that are familiar to collectors. I took Austin Dobson's *Eighteenth-Century Vignettes, Second Series,* off the shelf. It opened at this passage: "Lady Louisa Stuart was one of those writers whose silence is a positive misfortune to the literature of the *Memoir.* Living to a great age, for she died in 1851, at ninety-four, she had accumulated a store of memories, and she had inspected life with the keenest perceptions and with unusual advantages of position. . . . It was she who wrote the introduction to Lord Wharncliffe's edition of the letters of her grandmother, Lady Mary Wortley Montagu—an introduction which sparkles with unpublished eighteenth-century anecdote of the most brilliant character, *and she contributed many of the more interesting notes to the Selwyn Correspondence.* . . . It is not too much to say that, in some respects, Lady Louisa could give points even to that inimitable gossip Horace Walpole himself." The words I have italicized sent me hurrying down to New Haven on the following morning to get advice and help; the last sentence lingered in my mind.

The question was: had Lady Louisa's notes on the Selwyn correspondence been published? Austin Dobson's remark seemed to indicate that they had been, but he might have seen them in manuscript. Professor Chauncey Brewster Tinker suggested that I find out about The Hirsel, from the library of which Lady Louisa's notes had come; Mr. Andrew Keogh, the University Librarian, suggested that I look through *Notes and Queries,* a periodical I discovered to my dismay had been in existence for upwards of eighty years. The library had the books Austin Dobson referred to and others by Lady Louisa, but it took me months to find out that a selection of her remarks on the Selwyn Correspondence that I owned had been printed as footnotes by James A. Home in his pri-. vately printed *Letters and Journal of Lady Mary Coke,* that The Hirsel was the seat of his brother, the Earl of Home, and that Lord Home had recently sold some books, among them my copy of Jesse's *Selwyn.* Meanwhile I had encountered over and over again the name of Horace Walpole.

SIR ROBERT AND LADY WALPOLE

II

Horace Walpole was born in 1717, the third and youngest son of Sir Robert Walpole, the Prime Minister. The outline of his life followed the eighteenth-century upper-class pattern: Eton, King's, the Grand Tour, Parliament, a town house, a country house, a round of expensive diversions with other rulers of the first British Empire. He never married. Was he ever in love? Yes, I think so, perhaps three times: in his youth, middle age, and old age. His sole affair seems to have been with "the finest woman in Florence," Mme Grifoni, whom he met on the Grand Tour.

He was brought up by his mother who was on such bad terms with his father that even today gossip has it that his real father was not Sir Robert Walpole, but Carr, Lord Hervey, the brother of Pope's "Sporus, that mere white curd of ass's milk." When Lady Walpole died, in Horace's twentieth year, he sank into a profound melancholy, from which Thomas Gray and his closest friends had difficulty in rousing him. Her death occurred while he was at

Cambridge, where he lived in the fitful residence then permitted to the sons of the rich and powerful. His life may be said to have begun again two years later when he took Gray with him as his companion on the Grand Tour. They came home by separate routes (Europe has always been strewn with the wrecks of friendships), but the two years spent in France and Italy, chiefly in Florence with Horace Mann, the British envoy, gave lasting benefits to both. They subsequently resumed their friendship and continued it, unclouded, until Gray died.

When Walpole got back to England in 1741, he found himself a Member of Parliament. His father's long Premiership was drawing to a close. During its final dramatic scenes in the House Sir Robert and he became fast friends instead of virtual strangers. Sir Robert's fall made little difference to Horace, "the friend of London," so far as his enjoyment of life went, for as long as he lived he was as much in the center of things as he chose to be. He sat in Parliament twenty-six years. While there his gifts for faction and maneuver were used not for his own advantage, but for that of his cousin, Henry Seymour Conway.

His money, a considerable sum for a younger son, came from the places in the Exchequer that his father gave him. He had all the money he wanted to spend on his house and collections; he was never in the slightest financial trouble, for he kept his expenses prudently within his income. He gambled for stakes that seem high to us today with the ultra-respectable matrons and dowagers who made up his set, but gambling, which ruined so many eighteenth-century men and women, was never a passion with him; furthermore, he seems to have had extremely good luck. He was temperate in all things except collecting.

In his own day he was best known—apart from being the great Prime Minister's son—as an author of many books, the founder of the first eighteenth-century private press, and the creator of Strawberry Hill, which was famous alike as a revival of the Gothic taste and for its contents, which made it a museum known throughout Europe. He was a prolific author. Five of his books were pioneer works: *Ædes Walpolianæ: or, a Description of the Collection of Pictures at Houghton Hall in Norfolk, the Seat of the Right Honourable Sir Robert Walpole, Earl of Orford* (1747); *A Catalogue of Royal and Noble Authors of England, with Lists of their Works* (2 volumes, 1758); *Anecdotes of Painting in England* (5 volumes, 1762–71); *The Castle of Otranto* (1765); *Historic Doubts on the Life and Reign of King Richard the Third* (1768).

In 1791 he succeeded his mad and debt-encumbered nephew as Earl of Orford. This unwanted estate involved him in business and lawsuits, which he conducted with skill, in spite of his age and the gout. When he died, March 2, 1797, he had already become a legend.

What kind of man was he? "Countless writers have discussed him," Lord David Cecil has recently said, "but at the end all have confessed themselves baffled." To Lord David he is "more like a sprite than a man," with "his dragonfly elegance"; Virginia Woolf found him "the strangest mixture of ape and cupid that ever was"; Macaulay, "a pâté-de-foie-gras . . . made of livers preternaturally swollen." Croker said that he was a poisoner of history at its source; Saintsbury that he was the key to society; Carlyle that he was "a small, steady, light . . . unusually accurate . . . an irrefragible authority"; Byron, that he was "surely worthy of a higher place than any living writer, be he who he may." One is reminded of the blind Indian philosophers who said what an elephant was after each had felt a different portion of its body.

This bafflement of the critics is not surprising, for contradictory qualities abound in Walpole. As a boy he was so sickly that he was not expected to live, yet he lived into his eightieth year; though a *petit-maître*, he hardened himself by walking out of hot rooms into the cold without putting on a coat. When

To Mr Bull from M. & A. Berry

HORACE WALPOLE IN THE LAST YEAR OF HIS LIFE

the monument to his mother was put up at Westminster Abbey, he was afraid to go alone among the schoolboys there to see it; yet when his friend Lord Lincoln was threatened by two drunken officers at the opera, he clambered over the intervening boxes and chairs to go to his aid. He was a good man of business whose head was filled with romantic visions; a man of the world with a passionate concern for the underdog; a placeman of scrupulous honesty; a politician who declined the fruits of victory. He was a shrewd critic of Shakespeare who saw in William Mason another Pope; the best "eye" of his time for pictures who found the etchings of Lord Harcourt sublime.

Friendship accounts for these last two aberrations. Walpole had a gift for friendship: he was at home with all ages; with the scholarly Cole and the dissolute Rigby, with the manly Conway and the effeminate Chute, with the cynical Selwyn and the pious Hannah More, with just about everyone except opponents of his father. He was not a profound thinker; rather, he was a man of strong and partisan feeling. His friends who dabbled in letters and the arts were one and all geniuses, whether they were Thomas Gray or Mrs. Damer. All writers on the other political side—Johnson notably—were mountebanks. (The niceties of criticism rarely rose above faction in that age.)

He befriended the underdog throughout his life. When Admiral Byng was court-martialed and condemned to death, Walpole moved heaven and earth to save him; when his cousin Henry Conway was deprived of his regiment, he helped restore him to favor. He refused to testify against Maclean, the highwayman who had robbed him, even though Maclean's pistol had gone off accidentally and the ball had so narrowly missed Walpole that his face was pockmarked with powder. He raised money to release "King Theodore" of Corsica from a debtors' prison. He paid for the publication of the expensive *Designs by Mr. R. Bentley for Six Poems by Mr. T. Gray* to advance the reputation of his two friends; and to help Raspe, the author of *Baron Munchausen,* he paid for his *Critical Essay on Oil-Painting.* He printed one book at the Strawberry Hill Press for the benefit of Mr. Hill, a learned but indigent tailor; he printed a second to allay the misfortunes of the Reverend Mr. Hoyland, the decline of whose body and mind prevented him from accepting a living and comfort in South Carolina; the elaborate Strawberry Hill edition of Lucan's *Pharsalia* was printed to pay Bentley's debts; another Strawberry Hill publication was printed for the benefit of the poor of Twickenham, to whom he left three hundred pounds in his will. He would send guineas anonymously to sick prisoners or persons who advertised their need for help, if on investigation he was satisfied that they really were deserving objects of charity.

It is significant, I think, that Walpole did not become attached to his father until Sir Robert fell from power. Thereafter he was the champion of his father's reputation and the apologist for every act of his life. One of Sir Robert's natural daughters, Lady Mary Churchill, was Horace's favorite in his immediate family. He gave his name to one of her sons and stood godfather to various of her children and grandchildren; he left Lady Mary and her family generous bequests. When he discovered another of his father's illegitimate daughters, a Mrs. Daye, he took care of her until she died. A visitor to Strawberry Hill describes her as being of a "squab, short, gummy appearance," and with scarcely more agreeable qualities of mind. She could not have been a brilliant addition to Horace Walpole's dinner table, yet the man who has frequently been called a snob made his home her own. Another resident of Strawberry Hill was Mrs. Leneve, who had been a governess in his father's household. No two men were apparently more dissimilar than Horace Walpole and Samuel Johnson, but they held in common many opinions and qualities, not the least admirable of which was the willingness to share their houses with derelicts of society.

The statement of a neighbor is a tribute not only to Walpole's goodness of heart, but to his gifts as a housekeeper: "As a master, he was loved by all his domestics—a change in his establishment would have excited the wonder and curiosity of all Twickenham."

Walpole took up traduced figures of history in the same way that he espoused contemporary victims of injustice. In his *Historic Doubts on the Life and Reign of King Richard the Third* he even tried to prove that Richard had been accused by Lancastrian historians of murders that, Walpole believed, he had not committed. His heroes were Lord Russell and Algernon Sidney, the intellectual patriots, "that sealed their integrity with their blood," as he put it.

His sympathy for the persecuted extended beyond individuals to groups and nations. He was one of the first Members of Parliament to come out against the slave trade on moral grounds. He did this in 1750, nine years before Wilberforce was born. *"We,* the British Senate, that temple of liberty, and bulwark of Protestant Christianity," he wrote, "have this fortnight been pondering methods to make more effectual that horrid traffic of selling Negroes. It has appeared to us that six-and-forty thousand of these wretches are sold every year to our plantations alone! —it chills one's blood. . . . We reproach Spain, and

STRAWBERRY HILL FROM THE SOUTH

yet do not even pretend the nonsense of butchering these poor creatures for the good of their souls!" When the workmen at Strawberry Hill went on strike and left him "up to the knees in shavings," he asked: "How can one complain? The poor fellows, whose all the labor is, see their masters advance their prices every day, and think it reasonable to touch their share." There was no more earnest supporter of the American Revolution. On the outbreak of the French Revolution he shifted his sympathy from the people to their victims. Macaulay cited this to prove the flimsiness of Walpole's republican sympathies. What Walpole's shift proved was his detestation of violence and injustice whether the perpetrators of it were high or low; he had nothing against good kings and popes; quite the contrary.

Walpole's long life was full of incidents furnished by his causes, his writings, guests, and correspondents. He accomplished a great deal. He made "the Gothic revival" popular by building Strawberry Hill and by writing *The Castle of Otranto*. He gave great impetus to the study of English antiquities and fine arts. His major accomplishment was writing the history of the eighteenth century in his memoirs and the letters where he gives us this history in his famous set-pieces —the execution of the rebel lords, the burial of

George II, the house-party scenes—and in ten thousand smaller accounts of the day-by-day life and thought of the time. These letters were written to carefully selected correspondents, who kept them for posterity.

In this country Horace Walpole has belonged to the English departments of our universities, who claim him as a letter-writer and the author of *The Castle of Otranto*. If we must have these unnatural segregations, the historians have as good a claim to him. The history that Horace Walpole wrote is a different sort of history from that written by his contemporaries Hume, Gibbon, and Robertson. To find a historian closer to him in spirit we must go to a writer of the next century whose works are listed in the libraries under quite a different classification. I mean Anthony Trollope. "The novel," Henry James reminds us, "is history." No two men were more unlike than Horace Walpole and Trollope: the one a small man to whom the words "elegant" and "ingenious" were applied in his day, a man who enjoyed such unmasculine tastes as iced water, pots of tuberoses, and the society of old ladies; the other a big-fisted, bearded, civil servant who rode to hounds. Yet both men gave to posterity a host of men and women who are more real to their readers than most people those readers have known. Trollope's St. James's

Street is separated from Walpole's by a hundred years, ours from Trollope's by nearly as long, but so great is the similar art of these two historians that we walk that significant thoroughfare in their company with confidence and understanding.

III

I

COLLECTORS are led on from book to book and from person to person. Lady Louisa Stuart led me to her contemporaries the Misses Mary and Agnes Berry, and they led me to Horace Walpole, who had introduced them to society. And so it was that when on the 28th day of February 1924 I wandered aimlessly down Chancery Lane and into Hodgson's, the auctioneers, and found a handsome set of Walpole's *Anecdotes of Painting in England* and six of his letters to John Pinkerton, the Scottish antiquary, that were to be sold in the Milnes Gaskell Sale on the following day, I decided I would like to have them. One volume, at least, of the *Anecdotes* had been given to its owner by Walpole; the margins of all five volumes were covered with manuscript notes that I immediately concluded were in the hand of Walpole. This was heady: an author's copy of his own book impresses even non-collectors. The letters were written in a neat, legible hand. It would be nice to have six letters of the most famous letter-writer in the language? The following day the books and letters were mine. I didn't really look at these purchases until months later. Then the most superficial comparison of the notes in the margins of the *Anecdotes* with Walpole's letters to Pinkerton showed that the notes were not in his hand. Exuberance and imagination had undone me. Nevertheless, the red morocco binding was very handsome; the books themselves, printed at the Strawberry Hill Press in quarto with many prints, were attractive; I hadn't done too badly.

My comparison of the two handwritings forced me to read my six Walpole letters with attention. One of them in particular struck me. This is it:

STRAWBERRY HILL,
July 31, at night, 1789

Dear Sir,

Having had my house full of relations till this evening, I could not answer the favour of your letter sooner; and now I am ashamed of not being able to tell you that I have finished reading your Essay on the Ancient History of Scotland. *I am so totally unversed in the story of original nations, and I own always find myself so little interested in savage manners, unassisted by individual characters, that though* you *lead me with a firmer hand than any historian through the dark tracts, the clouds close round me the moment I have passed them, and I retain no memory of the ground I have trod. I greatly admire your penetration, and read with wonder your clear discovery of the kingdom of Strathclyde—but, though I bow to you, as I would to the founder of an empire, I confess I do not care a straw about your subjects, with whom I am no more acquainted than with the ancient inhabitants of Otaheite. Your origin of the Picts is most able; but then I cannot remember them with any precise discrimination from any other hyperborean nations: and all the barbarous names at the end of the first volume, and the gibberish in the Appendix was to me as unintelligible as if I repeated Abracadabra, and made no impression on me but to raise respect of your patience, and admire a sagacity that could extract meaning and suite from what seemed to me the most indigestible of all materials. You rise in my estimation in proportion to the disagreeable mass of your ingredients. What gave me pleasure that I felt, was the exquisite sense and wit of your introduction, and your masterly handling and confutation of the Macphersons, Whitaker, &c., there and through your work. Objection I have but one; I think you make yourself too much a party against the Celts—I do not think they were or are worthy of hatred.*

Upon the whole, dear Sir, you see that your work is too learned and too deep for my capacity, and shallow knowledge. I have told you that my reading and

Strawberry hill
july 31. at night
1789

Dear Sr

having had my house full of relations till this Evening, I coud not answer the favour of yr Letter sooner; & now I am ashamed of not being able to tell you that I have finished reading your Essay on the ancient history of Scotland. I am so totally unversed in the story of original Nations, & I own always find myself so little interested in savage manners, unassisted by Individual Characters, that tho' you lead me with a firmer hand than any Historian thro' the dark tracks, the clouds close round me the moment I have passed them, & I retain no memory of the ground I have trod. I greatly admire yr penetration, & reddle with wonder yr clear discovery of the kingdom of Strathclyde – but tho' I bow to you as I woud to the founder of an Empire, I confess I do not care a straw about yr subjects, with whom I am no more acquainted than with the ancient Inhabitants of Otaheite. your Origine of the Piks is most able; but then I cannot remember them with any precise discrimination from any other Hyperborean Nation: And all the barbarous Names at the end of the first Volume & the Gibberish in the Appendix was to me as unintelligible as if I repeated Abracadra, & made no impression on me but to raise respect of yr patience, & admire a Sagacity that coud extract meaning & suite from what seemed to me the most indigestable of all materials. you rise in my estimation in proportion to the disagreable mass of yr Ingredients.

WALPOLE TO PINKERTON, JULY 31, 1789

*knowledge is and always was trifling and superficial,
and never taken up or pursued but for present amusement. I always was incapable of dry and unentertain-
ing studies; and of all studies, the origin of nations
never was to my taste. Old age and frequent disorders
have dulled both my curiosity and attention, as well
as weakened my memory: and I cannot fix my attention, to long deductions. I say to myself, "What is
knowledge to me, who stand on the verge, and must
leave any old stores as well as what I may add to
them; and how little could that be?"*

*Having thus confessed the truth, I am sure you
are too candid and liberal to be offended; you cannot
doubt of my high respect for your extraordinary abili-
ties—I am even proud of having discovered them of
myself without any clue. I should be very insincere,
if I pretended to have gone through with eagerness
your last work, which demands more intense attention than my age, eyes, and avocations will allow. I
cannot read long together; and you are sensible that
your work is not a book to be read by snatches and
intervals, especially as the novelty, to me at least, requires some helps to connect it with the memory.
With the same truth with which I have spoken now,
I am, dear Sir,*

Yr sincere admirer and friend,

Hor. Walpole

After reading and pondering my six letters I read all of Walpole's letters in print. The standard edition of them was Mrs. Paget Toynbee's. It filled fifteen octavo volumes, each of about four hundred and fifty pages; a sixteenth volume contained the index. After Mrs. Toynbee's death three supplementary volumes were edited by her husband. The letters in their edition are arranged chronologically. They begin with the letter Horace Walpole wrote in his eighth year to his mamma; they end with the letter Lord Orford wrote in his eightieth year to Lady Ossory. The earliest letter shows his devotion to his mother, his relations, friends, and pets, and mentions that he is dining out on the following day; the last letter finds him begging Lady Ossory not to praise his letters and to spare him from further writing, which he was too weak to do himself.

At home [he dictated] *I see only a few charitable elders, except about four-score nephews and nieces of various ages, who are each brought to me about once a year, to stare at me as the Methusalem of the family. . . . Pray send me no more such laurels, which I desire no more than their leaves when decked with a scrap of tinsel and stuck on twelfth-cakes that lie on the shop-boards of pastry-cooks at Christmas. I shall be quite content with a sprig of rosemary thrown*

*after me when the parson of the parish commits my
dust to dust. Till then, pray, Madam, accept the resignation of your*

> *Ancient servant,*
> *Orford*

Between this letter and the one written seventy-two
years earlier were more than three thousand letters
on just about every subject of interest to the men and
women of the time.

Until I read Walpole's letters the eighteenth century had meant to me George Washington by Gilbert
Stuart, the Spirit of '76, a revival of *She Stoops to
Conquer* at prep school (in which I played the part,
to considerable applause, of Miss Constance Neville),
pretty china, and furniture. The eighteenth century
was a fancy-dress affair with everyone giggling in wigs
and tights, all except Dr. Johnson, who rolled about
on his bottom and said: "Too-too-too." Walpole's
letters changed all that. Thanks to him and Lady
Louisa Stuart, the men and women in Reynolds's and
Gainsborough's pictures stepped out of their frames
and became real people.

This sense of flesh-and-blood reality was, I think,
the first thing that struck me in Walpole's letters. At
school and college the people of other ages had only
been people in books, pressed between leaves, mythi-

cal creatures about whom I would presently be examined by instructors who (with a few notable exceptions) did not believe in their existence, either. The young man who made the eighteenth century come alive for me was, at the end of Volume I of his collected letters, just my age, twenty-eight. He made me feel that I was at his elbow. It is a short step from being at the elbow of a character in history or fiction to being the man himself.

But before taking this step I had to be satisfied that certain charges frequently made against Walpole were untrue. One of these was that he quarreled with all his friends. That this was not so is plain to anyone who reads his letters. His capacity for lasting friendship was one of his most endearing qualities. He took more than his share of the blame for his quarrel with Gray, I thought, and later rebuilt their friendship; his coolnesses with Montagu and Mason were easy to understand, for they discouraged him from writing to them by not answering his letters or answering them in a perfunctory way. Over against these failures— which were remarkably few in the life of a gregarious man who lived to his eightieth year—could be put scores of friendships that were never impaired. Far from being a quarrelsome person, it was clear that Horace Walpole was uncommonly loyal and patient.

Then there was the charge that he had been heartless to Mme du Deffand, the "blind old debauchée of wit," who presided over the most brilliant salon in Paris and who fell in love with him. She was sixty-eight and he twenty years younger when they met. Walpole was unkind to her, critics have said, on the basis of her complaints to him; he scolded her, he repulsed and neglected her. Since all but seven of his more than eight hundred letters to her were destroyed, we have little to go on but the unsubstantiated charges of an *exigeante* and passionate woman. He once wrote that he had "scolded her black and blue" when she played a practical joke on him, and I was glad that he had. He was undoubtedly aware of the comic aspect of their situation (which was platonic, much to her annoyance), and since he knew that their letters were opened at the post and copied, I did not blame him for being embarrassed by her infatuation for him or for dreading the consequences of its being disclosed to a society that throve on ridicule. Nor did I think much of the charge of neglect: he dragged himself four times, in spite of the gout, over to Paris, enduring the discomforts of the Channel, the roads, and French inns, that he might give her pleasure.

The most serious charge against Walpole has been that he was responsible for Chatterton's suicide. The story has been told over and over again. Chatterton, aged sixteen, sent Walpole, the historian of English painting, an account he had fabricated, "The Ryse of Peyncteynge yn Englande, wroten bie T. Rowleie, 1469 for Mastre Canynge." Walpole, aged fifty, replied courteously, thinking that his correspondent was still another unknown antiquary. Chatterton, delighted, then sent Walpole some verses of his composition that he said were also of the fifteenth century and told Walpole that he was "an apprentice with a taste and turn for more elegant studies" who hoped that Walpole would help him pursue them. Walpole was struck by the verses, but, after conferring with Gray and Mason, he became convinced that the manuscripts were forgeries; which they were. He sent Chatterton a kind and avuncular letter; Chatterton, who was both a genius and a thoroughly unpleasant youth, wrote a furious letter demanding his verses back. Walpole was about to set out for a six weeks' visit to France and did not return the verses until he got back. Chatterton killed himself two years later, in 1770, after he had gone to London and addressed himself to several other persons.

In 1778, in the Preface to Chatterton's *Miscellanies in Prose and Verse*, Walpole was accused by its editor of having through his "neglect and contempt . . . deprived the world of works which might have contributed to the honour of the nation." Walpole answered the editor in a long letter, which he printed at Strawberry Hill. So far as I was concerned, Walpole's reply was completely convincing. The most competent judges in every generation, including Walpole's own, have called the charge absurd, but it will never die because it is too romantic: there will always be those who want to think of Horace Walpole as a cold-blooded aristocrat driving a poor young genius to despair. Recently an indignant essay on the subject by the youthful Browning has come to light. Wordsworth called Chatterton "the Marvellous Boy . . . that perished in his pride"; Coleridge wrote a "Monody on the Death of Chatterton," in which he referred to "the bleak freezings of neglect"; Shelley, Keats, and Rossetti wrote verses to the memory of Chatterton; Alfred de Vigny wrote a tragedy about him. I could not have collected Walpole if I had believed that he had been the cause of Chatterton's death. When I became convinced that Walpole was no more responsible for it than I was, I turned to my friend and guide in such matters, Professor Tinker. "Instead of being just a gossipy little dilettante, isn't Horace Walpole one of the major figures of the eighteenth century?" I asked. "Yes," he replied. "And hasn't he been greatly undervalued?" "Yes," said Tink. So Walpole, the champion of the underdog, was himself in need of a champion.

2

Although I did not realize it, I had reached the fork in the road that leads, on the one hand, to specialized collecting and, on the other, to general collecting. Collectors reach this fork fairly early in their journey. The decision is usually made instinctively. As a ten-year-old collector of stamps I had specialized in the Hawaiian Island Provisional Government issue of 1893. Now I was at the fork in the road again. Should I pursue the broad highway that continued to English literature in general or turn off on the narrow, weed-grown road that led to Horace Walpole?

At just that moment the Beverly Chew Sale took place in New York. In it was Walpole's copy of Gray's *Odes,* the first book Walpole printed at his private press, with a few notes in his hand. With it was Garrick's "Ode to Mr. Gray," which was also printed at Strawberry Hill, in what the catalogue said was an edition of six copies. These were items a collector who was being drawn into the eighteenth century could not ignore. I went down to New York to see them.

On the way to the Anderson Gallery I met the lady who three years later became my bride. She was walking two Scotties, Ginger and Jamie, and we all went to look at the Walpoliana. I asked at the office what they thought the *Odes* would bring, and was told four thousand dollars. This meant that collecting Horace Walpole was not for me. My future wife and her Scotties went uptown and I strolled, mournfully, down Fifth Avenue. At Scribner's I paused, debating going in, and started on, only to be stopped by the occult force that guides collectors. It led me into the shop and up the stairs to the mezzanine floor, where the old books were then kept. Had they any books from the Strawberry Hill Press? Yes, they had a nice copy of Gray's *Odes* and the rare Garrick leaflet, one, they said, of six copies. Also they had a little collection of eight other "detached pieces" from the Press. The price? One hundred and fifteen dollars for the lot.

I said I'd think about it and walked back to the University Club, where I was lunching with one of my brothers. "There is no point in my buying those things," I said to my brother, "and stopping there. If I buy them I shan't stop until I have the finest collection of Walpole in the world."

This was the valor of ignorance; I hadn't the faintest idea of what I was talking about. I didn't know how many books and leaflets were printed at the Strawberry Hill Press—and of course nothing of the forgeries and reprints of them—or how rare some

45

of them are. I did not know how many books, pamphlets, essays, and verses Walpole wrote, let alone whether or not the manuscripts of them and his letters existed in any number. As for the contents of Strawberry Hill, the books in its libraries, the prints, pictures, enamels, curiosities, medals, coins, china, furniture, and objects of art that crowded its walls and rooms to the amazement and edification of Europe, all that was equally unknown to me. I did not know what collections, great or small, existed of Walpole, or whether he was actively collected; that is, what competition, if any, I should have. I was completely unaware of the vastness of the subject and the difficulties that lay in the way of attaining supremacy in it. This was fortunate, for had I known, I should not have had the temerity to make the attempt. Yet when I talked about the greatest collection of Walpole in the world I must have sounded impressive, for my brother looked grave.

"Well," he said, "it's your own money, but I hope you won't do this."

So, as soon as lunch was over, I went back to Scribner's and bought the lot.

IV

I

THE FIRST STEP taken, I promptly took the second. This was to search the bookshops of New York for Walpoliana.

Logically, I suppose, when you begin to collect an author you should arm yourself with a bibliography of his work, including all the books and articles about him, and run them down, one by one. Instead of doing so, I blundered into every bookshop I saw and asked: "Have you any Horace Walpole?" Almost always the bookseller would look blank. "Horace Walpole," he would say, and then again: " Horace Walpole," as if the repetition might summon Walpoliana to his shelves. (In England, later, the bemused bookseller would say: "Horace Walpole; no, I'm afraid not; no, no Horace Walpole.") But I usually knew when I entered the shop whether there was anything in it for me, just as I am told snake-charmers know whether there is a snake in a clump of grass. If I felt that there was something, I would say that I'd like to look around and would wander off by myself. I

always found a book, manuscript, or print that I
wanted; usually the bookseller would hurry up with
a belated discovery of his own.

In the middle of February 1925 I went to London,
where for six weeks I haunted the far more numerous
and rewarding shops. The only lasting regrets that
the collector has are caused by his failure to buy an
item that belongs in his collection. I have nothing to
regret during those six weeks, when I got everything
I could find that referred to Walpole. This was a
great deal. The books he wrote and printed were
issued in small editions, but because few people collected Walpole, I found copies of most of them within
the first year. Fortunately, I early realized that one
copy of the first edition was not enough and that I
must have at least one example of every subsequent
edition. All books about Walpole I also bought; in
fact, the mention of his name in a book was enough
for me to buy it. This rule I presently extended to
his friends and to the subjects that I knew he was
interested in—the books he read and drew upon for
his letters and work. I have made twelve subsequent
trips to London to collect Walpoliana, but no later
year has yielded as rich a harvest for my library as
that visit in 1925. This wholesale buying proved to
be, in the light of later developments, wise.

Booksellers are business men, but they are also

scholars and teachers. Their learning, which is often prodigious, includes an understanding of persons who have the *bibliomanie*. Any bookshop might place over its door the inscription on the proscenium of the old Lampson Lyceum at Yale: "Here we learn not studies, but life." Two London booksellers made special contributions to my education as a collector.

2

In February 1924 I had met in London a bookseller so well known that he is called "X" in print. He was a large man with a soft voice and cockney accent. He induced bibliomania by hypnotism and spells.

I succumbed completely to X. Books and prints filled the shelves of his shop and covered the walls throughout the dozen small rooms and passageways; you had to pick your way over and around books on the floor and on the dark, narrow stairs. Mr. X led me up a flight, cautioning me solicitously to mind the turns and the books on the turns, to the "special" room. A glass case ran along one wall of it. In it were first editions of the nineteenth-century poets and the nineteenth-century novelists "in parts." The manuscript of Trollope's *Miss MacKenzie* was lying about for anybody to pick up for two hundred pounds. On the walls were original drawings by Leech and

Thackeray. But it was hard to look at anything, for X's flow of reminiscence demanded respectful attention. "Excuse me, sir," he would interrupt, with his gray appraising eye upon me, "but that chair you're sitting in—many's the time I've seen Mr. Swinburne sitting in it, or his friend Captain Burton. They would come here after a rather wild night out, I'm afraid. Mr. Meredith used to pop in and out, and Mr. Watts-Dunton came looking for Mr. Swinburne."

X taught me a great deal; in fact, few men have taught me more, in or out of the book trade. The golden world of books, it appeared, had a darker side, in which a discreet use of artifice and even guile was required for survival. One must never, I learned, bid at English auctions oneself. To do so was not—well, if I would forgive the expression, not quite cricket. Gentlemen gave their bids to a member of the trade to execute for them, and it was just as well to keep the matter private. The ten per cent that the bookseller charged as a commission was a small charge, as gentlemen discovered when they made the serious— the very serious—error of bidding themselves, and Mr. X eyed me significantly.

X told me about the "knock-out," which he genteelly called "a settlement." Certain dealers, it seemed, did not bid against each other in "the rooms," but when the sale was over they retired to a public-house, constituted one of their number auctioneer, put up the lots they had bought for stock at the prices that they had fetched at the public auction, and continued the sale among themselves. The additional sum thus spent went into a pool that was divided among the participants. X made me feel that I had become an initiate in a trade whose duplicity was hidden behind an innocent mask.

X bid for me in the sale at Hodgson's that I have already mentioned, the Milnes Gaskell Sale, which had the six Walpole letters to Pinkerton and the beautiful set of *Anecdotes of Painting* with the contemporary manuscript notes. The Milnes Gaskell library was the finest I had ever seen; I felt that I had discovered it, and hurried to X to ask him to buy for me its beautiful copies of Ackermann's *Oxford* and *Cambridge,* with the *Founders,* the *Colleges,* the *Microcosm of London,* and Pyne's *Royal Residences,* as well as the Walpoliana, the most important of which I have not yet mentioned, the copy of Walpole's tragedy *The Mysterious Mother,* with William Mason's proposed alterations, which Mason had the effrontery to think improved Walpole's play. X and I went to Hodgson's separately on the 29th of February and we took no notice of each other while there.

The quiet of a London auction room, the speed with which the sale was conducted, the barnlike structure in which it took place, its chill (hats and coats were kept on most of the year), the inconvenient hour at which it was held (at one), were in marked contrast to American auctions. London auctions are strictly professional affairs. There are few excited amateurs who come in to bid on a single lot, the trade sees to that. It takes possession of the only chairs in the room. They are placed at tables arranged to form a rectangle in front of the auctioneer's rostrum. A porter of the firm stands inside the rectangle and walks around with the book that is being sold, handing it to any bookseller who wants to see it. The bidding is done by the slightest nod or lifting of a catalogue, and the books are sold without the haranguing and exhortation that make our auctions so tedious. "Fast selling is good selling," is a maxim of English auctioneers. Only when the auctioneer announced the purchaser did I know who had bought the lot, but X bought all of my lots, except one, at almost exactly the figure he said they would fetch. The one we lost was, unfortunately, Mason's copy of *The Mysterious Mother*.

This sale was memorable to me not only because it marked my first Walpolian purchases, but because of the presence at it of two persons, one of whom was Thomas J. Wise. He had come to see an uncut copy of *Adonais* sold. I had never heard of Wise before, but it was clear from the way he was regarded by everyone in the room that he was a person of the greatest consequence. It was ten years before John Carter and Graham Pollard exposed his forgeries of nineteenth-century poems and pamphlets; in February 1924 he was merely the greatest collector of modern English poetry in the world. He beamed indulgently when *Adonais* was knocked down to X for two thousand pounds, the highest price ever paid for a book at Hodgson's, as the auctioneer stopped the sale to announce. I never saw Wise again, but the other person who made the occasion memorable for me was the auctioneer himself, J. E. Hodgson. Years later he was to call my attention to many Walpole items, not only those that were to be sold in his rooms, but those he had found elsewhere. Auctioneers can be invaluable allies to collectors; such Mr. Hodgson has been to me.

When I got back to X's shop I found it in a state of jubilation, as a result of the *Adonais* victory. Reporters were interviewing X, photographers were taking his picture. He waved gaily to me as an old friend. "Well, sir," he said, "we carried the day before us. I am sorry we lost *The Mysterious Mother,* but we had to let Maggs have *something.*" He would not take the usual ten-per-cent commission from me on the lots that he had bought; securing such treasures for me was its own reward. Of course he did like cigars—I was not to be outdone in generosity: X was entitled to an eight-pound commission on the books he had bought for me at the sale. Accordingly, I was back in X's shop the next morning with a box of cigars that cost eight pounds. A dollar and sixty cent cigar is a princely cigar in any country, but not a bit too princely for such a royal bookseller as X. I felt that I had matched generosity with generosity, but X was too much for me. He had thrown out hints of the splendors of "the apartment" in which he and Mrs. X lived "right here on the premises." He gazed reverently at the cigars; then slowly raising his eyes he said: "I would be greatly honored, sir, if you would allow me to show you my apartment." It proved to be on the third floor, a large bright room filled with chintz. On a table in the center of the room in a tall silver vase was an enormous rose. "I am only a poor man," said Mr. X, " but I love beauty."

The climax of my friendship with X was reached when I asked him about some furniture on the top floor of the shop. "Oh, that, sir, that is not ordinary furniture. Those Sheraton chairs, that pair, belonged to Dr. Johnson."

"Dr. Johnson!" I looked at them with veneration.

"And that easel, that was Gainsborough's. This tea

caddy was Charles Lamb's, and this sofa pillow was worked by Mrs. Blake for Blake."

I was staggered. But I tried not to lose my head. "I confess, Mr. X," I managed to say, "my head is reeling. I don't want to sound extravagant, but everything in me is crying out: 'Get this furniture.'"

Mr. X was naturally pleased by my enthusiasm, and his pleasure added to it. But I had to be practical. "I haven't the slightest doubt about these things," I went on, "but you know how people are. What is their history?"

"Well," X replied roguishly, "I never saw Dr. Johnson sitting in them chairs."

"No, of course not," I laughed, "but where did they come from?"

He was serious again. "They belonged to a very distinguished gentleman, Professor Jackson, a great authority. When he died, the contents of his house were sold on the premises. They would have gone for nothing if I hadn't been there. I felt I should rescue what I could," and he told me again of his fondness, with which by now I was familiar, for the treasures of the past.

Professor Jackson, the friend of Pater and authority on Lamb (as X further informed me), was good enough for me, but I couldn't let it go at that. I conferred with a Johnsonian lady who thought the chairs must be all right, and streaked back to X's shop.

"I'll take them!" I said.

"There is just one little thing," Mr. X added after congratulating me on my decision, lowering his voice. "I'm a little short at the moment. If it wouldn't be too much trouble—"

"You mean money? Why, of course—"

"And one other thing, if you don't mind, sir. It's very old-fashioned of me, I suppose—" He paused and viewed me searchingly. "But why do I say this? Excuse me, please, sir."

"Go ahead, please!"

"Well, sir, I must tell you. I have enemies."

"Oh, no!"

"Yes, I have, sir. Excuse me for contradicting you, sir, but I have."

"What queer people they must be!"

"Thank you, sir. Thank you very much. It's American gentlemen like you, sir, who can understand how a person feels— But I mustn't trouble you with my private affairs."

"Please, Mr. X, won't you—"

"I was on the point of suggesting to you, sir, a moment back when I interrupted myself, in a manner of speaking." He chuckled. "I am getting on— oh, yes, I am, sir. I know it very well." At last the point was reached. Would I pay him in cash rather than by check?

I did so at once, two hundred pounds in notes, and then I asked myself just what had I got for my thousand dollars. I went to a friend I should have consulted earlier.

"Oh, my dear boy!" he said when I faltered out my tale. He gave me the name of a man who would certainly know about the chairs, and then, to make me feel better, he added: "The tea caddy *might* be all right. Jackson knew a lot about Lamb. But Jackson at the end was on the optimistic side in such matters; in fact"—he paused to let me have the full force of his next remark—"he was absolutely mad."

"Dr. Johnson? Sheraton?" The pince-nez of the furniture man glittered. "But Sheraton didn't make any chairs before 1790." And Dr. Johnson had died in 1784.

I screwed up my courage and returned to X. "About those chairs, Mr. X." The first hint of coolness appeared in his gray eyes. "I've decided not to take them, after all." He continued to regard me fixedly. "I believe that they were Dr. Johnson's, absolutely, but"—I didn't find it easy—"as you said, you never saw Dr. Johnson sitting in them."

"Just as you say, sir, of course. I told you you could return anything at any time."

"It's very generous of you. I am also returning Gainsborough's easel and Mrs. Blake's pillow. But," I added brightly, "I am keeping Lamb's tea caddy."

"Of course, sir, you are not expecting me to return your money?"

"Oh, no! I'll take something else."

This proved to be difficult. Either the prices of the books I looked at lacked the code initials that indicated their prices (the translation of which had been confided to me), or the initials no longer applied. Everything had gone up, had trebled and quadrupled. There was a marked drop in the warmth of our friendship. Reminiscence ceased altogether. I realized that I had become that bane of a shopkeeper's existence, the weak-minded customer who takes back the things he has bought.

It was therefore with relief that I stumbled over a large gray box and was told that it had belonged to Lewis Carroll. It contained fifty-two books and forty-four photographs of little girls (the inventory is before me), a box of wooden draughtsmen, two dice boxes, four dice, a small inlaid trick box, two match boxes, and one side of a match box, and I gratefully took it in exchange for what was left from the chairs, the easel, and the pillow.

When, however, in the following year I returned to England, the Lewis Carroll box preceded me. X's reception was very cool indeed. "Certainly, sir," he said, "I told you you could return anything at any time. You will remember that, sir. What will you have now?"

I was now, I explained, a collector of Horace Walpole and I should be glad to see whatever Walpoliana he had. I was told to return in a week, and when I did so, X had put out a few books, the most interesting of which was Walpole's copy of an obscure French book, worth, perhaps, ten shillings. The price of it was £60. "But, Mr. X," I protested, "I have just bought a large-paper copy of the King of Poland's *Works*, with Walpole's arms on the sides, for £4.10!"

"Very well, then," said X, and we were now not friendly at all, "thirty pounds. That's the kind of a man I am!" The furniture on the top floor was eventually transmuted into a few books priced at many times their current value.

On my next London visit I did not call on X, owing to a correspondence that temporarily suspended our relations, but I bought from him, through another dealer, the book I value above all others in my library, the architects' drawings for Strawberry Hill. In the following year, 1927, I returned to X, and ever after so long as he lived I paid him an early call on arriving in London.

He continued to turn up remarkable things for

me. Once, for example, he produced a colored drawing of an eighteenth-century boy of about ten years
of age. On the back of the drawing was written:
"Horace Walpole, afterwards Earl of Orford," in an
eighteenth-century hand. The day after I bought it
we went down to Somerset to visit the Waldegraves.
Lord Waldegrave is a descendant of Walpole's favorite niece, to whose son Walpole left Strawberry Hill
and its contents. Most of the contents had been sold
in 1842, but the Waldegrave family still had a large
Walpolian collection at Chewton Priory. Among the
books was a huge folio of Walpoliana collected by
Walpole's deputy at the Exchequer, Charles Bedford.
I turned a page, and there was a copy of the drawing
I had just bought from X. Beneath it, in the same
hand that appeared on the back of my drawing, Bedford had written: "from an original coloured drawing in my possession." Within twenty-four hours I
had found perhaps the only line of writing in existence that proved the authenticity of the drawing.

The last time I saw X he said with a smile as he
held my hand when I said good-by: "Oh, Mr. Lewis,
if I could get you on to another man!" But his teaching did not go that far.

THE COLORED DRAWING
OF HORACE WALPOLE AS A BOY

3

The lessons taught by A. W. Evans were of quite a different nature. His instruction was bibliographical and critical. It could be summarized: (a) buy books as near as possible to the condition in which they first appeared, and (b) any book published between 1740 and 1825 is a good book.

When I met Evans, in March 1925, he had just revived the old firm of Elkin Mathews at 4a Cork Street with two much younger partners who were also amateurs. It was a small shop filled with books printed between 1740 and 1825. The great majority of them were by forgotten authors. Early in this century the first editions of *Robinson Crusoe*, Gray's *Elegy*, Goldsmith's *Threnodia Augustalis*, the Kilmarnock Burns, and various Blakes were the only eighteenth-century books that fetched more than one thousand dollars at auction, and there were not many that fetched as much as one hundred dollars. At a guess, not one tenth of one per cent of the books published during the eighteenth century ever appeared in a West End catalogue. In Seymour de Ricci's *The Book Collector's Guide* (1921), which is an accurate picture of the collecting tastes of the time, Boswell and Johnson, Fielding, Smollett, and Sterne cut very modest figures. Walpole's only book to exceed one hundred dol-

61

lars was a copy of *The Mysterious Mother* "beautifully bound by Roger Payne." The eighteenth century was neglected by collectors and looked down upon by the Manchus of learning. The book world has its castes and classes, which were more rigidly defined then than they are now when the social revolution has overthrown such distinctions. The early books down to 1641 were the aristocracy; the eighteenth century, the bourgeoisie; and the bourgeoisie before 1914 had few champions.

During and after the First World War the eighteenth century came to life. A. E. Newton's *Amenities of Book Collecting* (1921) and C. B. Tinker's *Young Boswell* (1922) were the heralds of the resurrection in America; Lytton Strachey's essays and Saintsbury's *The Peace of the Augustans* (1916), in England. The middle of the twenties was just the moment for a shop to specialize in the eighteenth century, and Evans was just the man to conduct it. The catalogue that he and his partners issued in March 1925 is a milestone in collecting, for in it appeared eighteenth-century authors seldom seen west of Charing Cross Road since their deaths. Now they re-emerged in all the radiance of the revived Elkin Mathews, not for a few pence, but at prices that ranged from ten shillings to two guineas. William Mason, William Hayley, Anna Seward ("the Swan of Litchfield"), Ann Yearsley

("Lactilla, the Poetical Milkwoman"), John Gisborne ("the Man of Prayer"), and scores of others were raised from the dead.

Bliss was it in that dawn to be alive. In the back room of Elkin Mathews the eighteenth century was the sole reality; the election of President Hindenburg, Locarno, and slum clearance were subjects lost in the distance; the reason behind Dr. Johnson's efforts to save Dr. Dodd from the gallows was of present concern. (Evans had a theory about it—that Johnson and Dodd were Masons.) A young American who was consumed with zeal for the works and reputation of Horace Walpole was an object of interest to Evans. He disliked Walpole, who appeared to be the antithesis of Johnson, but Walpole did live in the eighteenth century and did write books. He was a pro-American Whig, and it was fitting that he should have a champion from America a century and a half after the Declaration of Independence. Walpole had feared and disliked Johnson and had called him "a saucy Caliban," but he did so out of loyalty to his friend Gray, whom, Evans acknowledged, Johnson had belittled. It was to Walpole's credit that he stood by his friend. Of Walpole's literary importance there was no question. In the world where Shenstone and Lyttelton and Soame Jenyns were notable figures, Horace Walpole was a colossus, whether you liked him or not.

I often had tea at 4a Cork Street. "Come in, come in," Evans would say; "a cup for Mr. Lewis, Miss Matson." A small clearing would be made among the books on the table. "Well, what have you found to-day?"

I had always found something. In 1925 books from Walpole's library and presentation copies of the Strawberry Hill Press publications were lying about in London shops. Evans would congratulate me gravely in his low, somewhat un-English voice. (What his accent was I never did make out, nor did I ever learn much of his life; Trinity College, Dublin, had come into it, I gathered, and, in spite of his Welsh name, he had the warmth we associate with the Irish.) His long, ascetic face would light up with pleasure. "That's good!" he would say; "you have bought an important book—and you got it cheap."

He gave me excellent advice. For one thing, he kept repeating that I should have all the editions of Walpole's letters. I was slow to grasp what seems obvious now. Evans had no editions of Walpole's letters in stock, but he kept urging me to get them until finally I realized that he must be right. In the next shop I went into (it was Hatchard's, the first time I ever went there), I found Mitford's own copy of his edition of Walpole's correspondence with William Mason, interleaved with Mitford's notes and letters about the work. Evans was overjoyed. When I said that it seemed too bad that he shouldn't make anything out of it, he replied: "That isn't important. What *is* important is that you should have the finest collection of Horace Walpole ever made, and I mean to help you get it." The coal smoke of London filtered into the shop and mingled with the smell of books and tobacco, and nothing mattered but the eighteenth century.

One of these conversations in March 1925 had far-reaching consequences. Evans told me that a great cache of Boswell manuscripts was reported by John Drinkwater to be at Malahide Castle, outside Dublin. The owner was a descendant of Boswell, Lord Talbot de Malahide. On getting home that year I repeated this news to Professor Tinker, who had heard rumors of Boswell manuscripts being at Malahide. That summer he went to Ireland and saw the manuscripts. He told A. Edward Newton about them and Newton told Colonel Ralph Isham. What happened next is now widely known. Evans's part in the most important and dramatic of all eighteenth-century finds was bookselling at its most disinterested.

Elkin Mathews prospered. New and affluent partners joined the firm; the old-fashioned shop in Cork Street was abandoned for a shop in Conduit Street expensively done up by Lord Gerald Wellesley (now

Duke of Wellington). Cinderella had gone to the ball. During this period of the firm's history Evans moped; selling Surtees in parts to the rich was less congenial than selling Warburton's *Divine Legation of Moses* in boards. Things got better when, during the depression, the firm was obliged to move to more modest quarters in Grosvenor Street, and better still when it had to give up its ground floor there and confine itself to the room above; Warburton fitted into reduced circumstances.

Once when I hurried around to see Evans on arriving in London, his recognition was startling. He stood up and, instead of greeting me as usual, said: "Horace Walpole was an insufferable cad!" adding darkly: "I shall be about the gallipots and washes of his toilet." This I recognized was what Warburton had said toward the end of his life when he suspected Walpole of laughing at him, and I rejoiced that Evans's book on Warburton was nearing completion. After he had delivered himself of this testament, Evans's conscience was cleared, and we had tea as usual. When his book appeared, there was nothing in it that could offend the most sensitive Walpolian.

Evans left the book world suddenly. When his wife died he returned to his profession, the Church, a profession I had not known was his, nor had I known that he was married. He spent his last days buried in

66

a parish in the south of England. Not only would he not come up to London, he would not reply to letters from his former associates. He would not have been more inaccessible if he had returned to the eighteenth century. With him, so far as I was concerned, went much of the pleasure and excitement of book-collecting in London.

Some years later I came upon a selection from the works of Carlyle that I had used in Freshman English. To my surprise, its editor was A. W. Evans. Although I had not realized it, he had been my teacher for half my life.

V

I

IN ADDITION to booksellers, the tyro has another set of teachers. This set is composed of other collectors, older collectors whose initial collecting ardors have perhaps cooled, but who still take collecting seriously. These older persons cannot tell the young collector what he should collect (only he can make that decision); they cannot tell him a great deal about how to collect (he must learn that by himself); but they can encourage him by example.

I never met the man who first helped direct (unconsciously) the course of my collecting. He was the Reverend Samuel McChord Crothers of Boston. He talked to the Thacher School one evening nearly forty years ago in the interval between supper and the evening study hour. Speakers on those occasions usually tried to save us from ourselves, but Dr. Crothers, even though he was a clergyman and an essayist, merely talked to us pleasantly about the delights of knowing another age as well as our own. A dozen years later Professor Tinker said something similar to

68

me one day and Dr. Crothers's little talk returned with the force of revelation.

My friendship with Tink goes back to the first class I walked into at Yale College in September 1914, a class in Freshman English. No more dramatic introduction to Yale College could have been devised. Although Tink had become a full professor (this class was the first he taught as one), he had not yet acquired a name that would have been known to every Freshman. At first I was stunned by so much brilliance, but as the year went on I found courage to raise my hand, and we became close friends. One of the reasons why I went back to Yale after the war was to take his "Age of Johnson."

During that year he and two of his colleagues in the English Department urged me to go into teaching. In 1920 recruits for the teaching profession were few—why should anyone drudge away on a professor's salary when you could be rich in no time by borrowing a little money and buying the right stocks? I saw myself teaching in the Tinkerian manner, but wouldn't I have to get a Ph.D.? Yes, it would be wise to get one, certainly; but there was no hurry about it, I could begin teaching at once and pick up my degree on the side. I was flattered by this invitation, but turned it down without hesitation. I *knew*, I said, that I could never become interested in research.

After two years on the staff of the Yale University Press I went to England, as I have described, and began collecting books. Tink had begun collecting at about the same time, keeping himself steadfastly to the period 1740–1910, from Richardson to Henry James. At this time he was more interested in the earlier books of the period than in the later, for this was when he was proving that Boswell, with all his shortcomings, was entitled to a much higher place in public esteem than he had been accorded. Boswell, as well as Walpole, had been a victim of Macaulay's reckless brilliance. What Tink had done showed how collecting, study, and conviction could alter an established reputation.

As already indicated, I often went down from Farmington to New Haven to talk to Tink and to get his advice, and he never gave me anything but the best advice. After I began collecting Walpole my visits became more frequent. At that time we talked of nothing but the eighteenth century, of how like our own time it was, of its use of words and phrases now obsolete, and what would happen to James Boswell if he found himself today at Fifth Avenue and Forty-second Street. "It is not easy," Tink said to me one day, "to populate a period with its people." I can see him now as he looked at me then, while we strolled down Hillhouse Avenue on a May afternoon. Could

I fill the eighteenth century with its people and see them moving about in it as they had lived? Doubtless I could not, but I knew that I was more interested in the people of the eighteenth century than in what they wrote, Walpole, Gray, Boswell, and Sheridan apart. Tink's remark coalesced in some way with Dr. Crothers's talk at school and made the study of the past—specifically, the eighteenth century—a job worth trying.

In January and February 1925 Tink gave me a forward push: he asked me to make a selection of Walpole's letters that he could use in the "Age of Johnson," and he asked me to lecture to the class on Walpole. These two assignments made my collecting something more than just a hobby; they made me feel that I was Tink's coadjutor in learned enterprise.

Harper's and the Oxford University Press brought out *A Selection of the Letters of Horace Walpole* in a textbook edition and an illustrated edition in two volumes. The illustrations came, for the most part, from unique material in my collection, and when I look at the illustrations now, I am surprised to find how much unique material I had acquired so early. The *Selection* was dedicated to Tink, of course.

Only once before had he ever invited a guest to lecture in the "Age of Johnson"; thus the honor conferred was marked. I got back from England a few days early in order that we might have a final conference. On the morning of my lecture he was as nervous as I was. We walked to A.1 Osborn Hall from his rooms in silence. Where did I want him to sit, on the right side of the aisle or on the left? When the class of about three hundred were seated expectantly, with me in Tink's chair on the platform, Tink stood in front of the first row of seats and introduced me. He talked, at the most, for half a minute in the easy, cadenced way of which he was (and is) a master. He concluded with a wave in my direction above him on the platform and a compliment that still infuses a glow.

Almost alone among university people Tink realized the importance of possessing the first editions of the books he studied and taught. Colleagues who said "The last edition is the best" with an air of having said something profound, he consigned to the pit without argument. How can you fully understand the effect of a book on its time unless you know what it looked like? he would ask (not the Philistines, he would not bother with them). Collecting, he would say, is a form of scholarship—exacting, imaginative, creative. Where, pray, would scholars be if there had been no collectors before them to bring together the books that make research possible? Collecting, libraries, publication, these three, and the first of these—

72

without which the other two would not exist—is collecting.

2

Paget Toynbee's fame rests chiefly on his Dante studies, but he will always have an honored place among Walpolians. When his wife died he gave up his own work to continue hers. He brought out three supplements to her edition of the letters and edited several other manuscripts that turned up after her death. There was never a keener Walpolian.

My friendship with him began in February 1925 when I sent him transcripts of the six letters that I had bought at the Milnes Gaskell Sale. That April I went down to see him at Burnham Beeches in his cottage at the meeting of five roads. The cottage had no electricity, no running water, of course no central heating, and no servant. When he felt like it, he had something to eat out of a tin or a box. A charwoman came in once or twice a week to wash up the tea things, but she was no trouble. He seldom left Fiveways, not even to go to the Bodleian, to whose "Friends" he contributed handsomely each year. He took pride in never having gone to Strawberry Hill, about which he had written so much and so well, although it was hardly an hour away. His last years (he was seventy when I first met him) were brightened by a robin that attached itself to him (quite literally

73

when it perched on his head) and became the subject of his letters to the *Times*. My wife and I sent the robin a bell. In return came Walpole's copy of Lucan's *Pharsalia* (1750).

I used to carry down to Fiveways books of special interest to show the anchorite, Bentley's drawings for Strawberry Hill and Walpole's extra-illustrated *Description of Strawberry Hill,* among them, which he explored with fascinated interest and infinite humor, but he observed that they "knocked out" much of his own work. As time went on I was disconcerted to discover that he began to regard me as something of a rival, and that the exchange of Walpolian information was becoming a one-way street. My modest *Selection of Walpole's Letters,* it seemed, had skimmed the critical cream. The eighteenth-century bigwigs in both countries had seized upon its appearance as an excuse to write essays on Walpole, so that when his own *Strawberry Hill Accounts* was published, it fell flat. He was not bitter about it; he just mentioned it as a fact, that's all. This may, unconsciously, have influenced him in regard to a somewhat more ambitious book that I was working on the last time I was at Fiveways. It was an edition of Walpole's fugitive verses. I understood that Lord Waldegrave owned three volumes of juvenilia that had many unpublished verses by Walpole. Toynbee had had the use of them,

THE HALL AND STAIRCASE AT STRAWBERRY HILL

I knew, for he had once told me that he had transcribed them, but all he said on that afternoon was, with a sly nod at a cabinet in the corner: "Ah! wouldn't you like to have a look in *there!*" When, fourteen years later, I acquired the manuscripts, it was plain how much better my book would have been if I had been able to include them in it. But the thick bundle of letters written in his neat small hand remains at Farmington, letters filled with friendly chat about Horace Walpole at a time when I needed it most, and I record my gratitude for many stimulating hours in his company, either while we wrote to each other three thousand miles apart or on those occasions at Fiveways when we crouched over the smoky coal fire or took a breather in the rose garden while his cape fluttered wildly in the cutting wind.

My other older Walpolian friend placed no such reserves upon his manuscripts. He was Percival Merritt, of Boston, who generously let me edit the two important manuscripts he owned. These were Walpole's "Paris Journals" and his "Book of Visitors" to Strawberry Hill. Merritt was the most active Walpolian collector in either country when I began my own collection. In his quiet, thoughtful way he was devoted to Walpole, and so was his wife. He published two or three pieces of Walpolian research, the most useful of which was a discrimination of the six different issues of the 1842 Strawberry Hill Sale Catalogue. I went up several times to see the Merritts in Marlborough Street, where, on the second floor, he kept his carefully chosen and tended Walpole collection. After his death his collection went by his desire to Harvard, but not before Mrs. Merritt sent me a much-coveted book from Walpole's library to remember them by.

3

R. W. Chapman wrote to me first in 1926. As the Secretary to the Delegates of the Oxford University Press he made it his business to keep in close touch with American scholars, and as a Johnsonian he was immediately aware when a new eighteenth-century collector appeared on the horizon. He first wrote to me about the bibliographical problem of the Additional Lives in Walpole's *Anecdotes of Painting*. I had no idea of the answer, but replied briskly—and we have been corresponding weekly ever since. The steps from "Dear Sir," "Dear Mr. Lewis," "Dear Lewis," "My dear Lewis," "My dear Lefty," were accomplished in the good time of three years. Hundreds of letters have gone back and forth between us. They get longer and longer as the years go by—and more and more cryptic. Even before the Second World War and the days of paper shortages Chapman wrote on the backs of proof and manuscript or any blank piece of paper that came to hand—receipted bills, calls to meetings, old proof sheets—and there is one sequence with little drawings of intestines on its versos, the biological exercises of his youngest son. Our friends are certain that whatever else the correspondence may be, it can have no rival in illegibility.

While stationed in Macedonia during 1917, Chapman wrote an essay that has found a permanent place in the literature of bibliophily, "The Portrait of a Scholar." The subject offered him an opportunity to show his own love of collecting and of books. "He [the subject of his essay] did not conceal a collector's just pride of possession; but you need only see him take a book from its shelf to know that he felt himself the ephemeral custodian of a perennial treasure. There is a right way and a wrong way of taking a book from the shelf. To put a finger on the top, and so extract the volume by brutal leverage, is a vulgar error which has broken many backs. This was never his way: he would gently push back each of the adjacent books, and so pull out the desired volume with a persuasive finger and thumb. Then, before opening the pages, he applied his silk handkerchief to the gilded top, lest dust should find its way between the leaves. These were the visible signs of a spiritual homage."

In the twenties and thirties Chapman and his colleague Sir Humphrey Milford used to cross the Atlantic every other year or so and would come to Farmington for a rest. Chapman would "review the shelves," going from book to book until he would murmur: "Ah!" Down would come the book, with due care for its back, and he would call: "Paper! Pen! Table!" While Milford and I played tennis or squash, Chapman would labor away on a bibliographical note that in due course would appear in the *Bodleian Quarterly Record* with the preface: "I have recently examined in the Walpolian collection of Mr. W. S. Lewis—"

At Farmington one day in 1929 I said to them: "Why don't you bring out a new edition of Walpole's letters?"

"Good lord!" said Milford.

Yet it was clear that the collectors and bibliographers of the twenties had added a great deal to the knowledge of the eighteenth century. Walpole's letters had often been printed, but never with anything like the editing necessary to make them clear to the modern reader. So we spoke about a new edition from time to time, calling it "1950," the remote year when it would be completed.

Chapman has done me countless kindnesses. When Paget Toynbee died, in 1932, he left his and his wife's correspondence about their edition of Walpole's let-

ters to the Clarendon Press for the use of any future
editor the press wished to encourage. At the proper
time Chapman handed over this correspondence
(which is invaluable) to me. He has read hundreds of
pages of proof and pointed out many slips that I and
my associates of the *Yale Edition of Horace Walpole's
Correspondence* would otherwise have made, but perhaps the greatest service of them all was the letter he
wrote in 1927 when he got my first attempt to com-
pile a scholarly work, a little notebook of Walpole's
that was reproduced in facsimile. My transcription of
it had numerous errors. Chapman listed them for me.
Then he wrote: "Really, my dear Lewis, it won't do!"

Ten years later he reviewed the first volumes of the
Yale Walpole for the [London] *Times Literary Supplement.* His review was given the front page, which
at that time was an accolade. "If the event," wrote
Chapman, "is equal to its promise, it may well eclipse
the Variorum Shakespeare as the greatest achievement
of editorial scholarship in the United States." Making all allowances for hyperbole inspired by friendship, he could not, I think, have written that review
had he not first written the letter.

4

No man expanded my youthful horizon more rapidly than the late Edward Clark Streeter, of Chicago,

Yale, Boston, and Stonington, Connecticut, the friend
of Osler, Welch, and Cushing, a beloved member of
the oldest and most eminent section of the biblio-
philic guild, the medical humanists.

From the moment I met Ned Streeter on the dock
at Southampton in 1925 (I was sailing home with a
classmate of his), I sensed that he was a collector of
note. This was confirmed during our first talk on ship-
board. He knew all the great booksellers not only of
London and Paris, but of Amsterdam, Munich, and
Florence as well. It was clear that I had hardly
reached the letter B in the alphabet of collecting as
he practiced it. Although I was rather full of my own
little successes in London, the too detailed recital of
which must have been a trial to him, he listened to
me with patience—with patience, I felt, but not with
complete approval. Then one day he came out with
his reservation: "What about the Marvellous Boy?"
he asked with the nearest approach to sternness I ever
saw in him. When I said that I had asked myself the
same question before starting my collection, and
showed him why Walpole was no more responsible
for Chatterton's death than I was, he took my word
for it.

After that conversation he invited me down to his
stateroom to see an object he had just acquired, the
only known Anglo-Saxon weight outside the British

Museum. King Alfred might have handled it. Ned
had discovered it some years before in the possession
of a clergyman in the south of England. An introduction was managed. Having gained admission to the
rectory, Ned forbore, with immense self-control, to
explore the possibility of the weight's passing into
his own keeping. A year or two later the rector's lady
developed signs of illness. What did Dr. Streeter rec-
ommend? Ned had been a surgeon before he gave up
practicing medicine to collect and write about medical history, yet it was plain to him that what the lady
needed was a warmer climate. Alas, the rector did not
have enough money for such a trip— When the
weight was finally shown me in the *Olympic,* the lady
and her husband were in Italy. Ned and his Anglo-
Saxon weight indicated extra-stellar spaces for the exercise of the collecting spirit.

The following year he and I went to England on a
collecting trip. We would go our several ways during the day. Ned listened in the evening with kindness and courtesy to the details of my finds, even
though they were only of books printed in the eighteenth century. Ned belonged to the élite of the book
world, as well as of the weight world. He had Caxtons
and Aldines, books from Grolier's library, incunabula
by the yard. He took an indulgent view of my collecting; better the eighteenth century than the nine-

teenth or twentieth, but why not go back to the real books? When one day I produced Walpole's copy of Blount's *Art of Making Devises* (1650), he was encouraged. "Ah!" he said, "that's better!" Although it was ten years too late for the *Short Title Catalogue of Books Printed in England, Scotland, and Ireland and of English Books Printed Abroad, 1475–1640,* and therefore not of the aristocracy, it was a highly respectable book, a year older than Jean Pacquet's *Experimenta Nova Anatomica.* "I have been trying to think," he went on, "of someone for you to collect, and now I've got him, Philipp Melanchthon!"

To me this formidable name was merely one among many encountered some years before in History A.1, "From the Fall of Rome to T. Woodrow Wilson." Ned launched into a gentle disquisition upon Melanchthon that proceeded to Luther and Wittenberg and the pomps and thunders of the Reformation, but to no avail. I only wanted to collect Horace Walpole and the eighteenth century.

Although Ned was disappointed, he continued to talk about Willibald Pirkheimer, Ambroise Paré, and Gui Patin and the copies of their works that he had bought in Paris and Bologna and Frankfurt. He was planning a paper on the French barber surgeons and their influence in spreading the use of the vernacular in medical treatises, a subject I found somewhat beyond me. Our talks took place in the smoking-room at Brown's Hotel, which we had to ourselves after dinner. We sat in semi-darkness, deep in leather chairs that crackled when we moved. The smoking-room waiter would cross the room with two brandies for someone in the drawing-room; the door from the pantry would sigh discreetly behind him; he would glance at us and no doubt wonder what there could be in it for this strange American pair who bought books and *weights* all day long and talked about them all night. Ned may then have been telling me the story of the perfidious Mme Belin. I should remember that story, for I heard it several times in the twenty-odd years of our friendship. It was, I think, about Gui Patin, a book he had in prison *(was he ever in prison?)*, or read the night before he went to the stake *(did he go to the stake?)*. The point of the story was that Ned had found this book in Mme Belin's shop, had bought it for a song, and then told her (boasting, I am afraid) what a bargain she had let him have. She was enraged and insisted that he return it to her. He, the mildest of men, had given it back. "But why?" I would ask. "I really don't know," was his answer. This story always depressed both of us, and we would go to bed.

A few years later Ned's great medical library—one of the finest ever made by an American—went to the

New York Academy of Medicine, via Dr. Rosenbach. This completed his separation from book-collecting; his energies were now concentrated upon weights and their companions, measures. By this time Ned knew more about such objects than anyone in the world. By inevitable progression they were dragging him on into an even larger field, pharmaceutical jars and accessories. He got together an Italian apothecary's shop of the sixteenth century and an early nineteenth-century southern New England shop. The last winters of his life were spent searching the antique and junk shops of the New York East Side with wonderful results, for only Ned Streeter was sure of what those lumps of lead and odds and ends had originally been. He came to Farmington all too rarely. When there, we would have a "Walpole Wallow" that always taught me—whatever avenue we explored—far more than it taught him, for his great and modest learning illuminated even what was most familiar to me.

The climax of our friendship came in 1939. Yale had decided to build a wing to its Medical School to house the historical collections of Harvey Cushing, Arnold Klebs, and John Fulton. The eyes of all concerned were upon Ned's weights and measures and apothecary shops. What was he going to do with them? Obviously, they should be in a library or mu-

seum; what more suitable place than the new Historical Library in the Medical School at Yale? Ned was
a Yale graduate; his rare and little-known collections
would join the books of his devoted friends; practi-
cally and sentimentally he could not do better than
give his collections to Yale.

The net closed in on him. One day that summer I
went to Stonington. "You know," I said, "there are
three stages in the preparation of prospective donors
for the sacrifice: Light Massage, Deep Massage, and
High Irrigation. You have had the first two for years."
He nodded. "Cush is expecting you at dinner next
Tuesday to get the third." I recall this conversation
very clearly. We had gone behind one of the red
barns to see an ancient painted ox-cart that Ned had
just got from Italy.

The following Tuesday he was at the Cushings' in
New Haven. We played croquet before dinner, Dr.
Cushing, Dr. Bayne-Jones, then Dean of the Medical School, Bernhard Knollenberg, then Librarian of
Yale, and I. Ned was not allowed to win; in fact, he
was not allowed to get through the second wicket.
(Yale has never babied its benefactors.) After dinner
the others went out on the porch, while Ned and I
lingered behind. When we joined them they were
bending over the blueprints of the new library. Ned
peered cautiously over their shoulders, and there

printed plainly for him to see were two fine rooms marked STREETER COLLECTION.

Two years later the Historical Library was opened. Dr. Cushing had died, Dr. Klebs was in Switzerland; Dr. Fulton was present and so were Dr. Bayne-Jones and Mr. Knollenberg; I presided. The crowd overflowed into adjoining rooms, for the occasion was a notable one in American medicine. Medical scientists had come from far and near to do honor to the memory of Cushing and to his coadjutors. "Didn't Ned Streeter come?" I asked in dismay. Yes, he was somewhere, but not where he should have been, not on the platform. He was not even in the front row. "This is carrying modesty too far," I thought, but not seeing him made it easier for me to pay the tribute that was due him. This I did in grateful remembrance of those nights at Brown's when he discoursed on the marvels of sixteenth-century medicine and showed me how pleasant learning can be. After the speaking was over I looked around for him. He was not in any of the rooms where the reception was being held. Then I went where I should have gone first. There he was, sitting quietly in one of the Streeter Rooms, beside the case in which was shown the only known Anglo-Saxon weight in the Western world.

VI

I

THE FIRST FINE books I ever handled were in the Elizabethan Club at Yale when, on Tuesdays, the vault was opened. My favorite was the first edition of *Paradise Lost* because of its binding, an olive-green affair with a gilt cypress tree on it. This was the work of an expensive London binder of the 1890's, and I had passed the first stage of my progress as a collector when I saw that, far from being an object of beauty, that binding was a blight upon the book. Even a binding by one of the great binders, I learned, was little better than a frill. "Why bother with husks?" Ned Streeter once asked me, a question that would certainly irritate the collectors of Mearne, Payne, Derome, and the rest.

I am not clear what were the next lessons that I learned. My experience with the draper's widow at Newbury taught me several—that "old" books are not necessarily valuable; that it is important to have one's books complete, not lacking title-pages and half-title-pages, or maps and prints that were issued with the books; that bargains are not often found in obscure shops. These matters were clear to me by the time I had begun collecting Walpole. By then I had also come to the stage usually reached early by collectors in their progresses, the stage where "association copies" have a particular attraction.

Association copies are the books given or owned by their authors or other persons of note. An example of an association item (about the best one I know) is a book in Professor Tinker's library, Glanvill's *Vanity of Dogmatizing* (1661), the copy given by Browning to Matthew Arnold, the very copy that moved Arnold to write "The Scholar Gipsy."

And near me on the grass lies Glanvill's book—
Come, let me read the oft-read tale again.

Lovers of association books, if they care anything for one of the most beautiful poems in the language, regard that copy with veneration.

Coincidence is so frequent in this branch of collecting that the collector of association items is led to believe that he has occult powers and that the person he is collecting is seeing to it that books, manuscripts, prints, snuffboxes, and so on, formerly in his possession come to the attention of the collector. This exciting possibility seemed confirmed in me in the spring of 1925 when Professor Tinker asked me, as I was leaving for England, to get him a first edition of Walpole's *Castle of Otranto*. I hadn't one myself at that time and said so. Mr. Tinker replied that he would be content with a good ordinary copy, and then, knowing my fondness for association books, he added: "And you can have the copy Walpole gave to William Cole." He said Cole rather than anyone else because Walpole's two most illuminating passages on *The Castle of Otranto* were written in letters to Cole, one of them going with a copy of the book. Apart from Walpole's copy it would probably be, from an association point of view, the most desirable copy in existence—if it still existed.

The first edition of *The Castle of Otranto* was of only five hundred copies. Since it has been the most sought-after of Walpole's books, I was lucky to find a copy of it in London; yet one copy for two collectors presented a problem. Should I let Mr. Tinker have the book or could I keep it for myself? After much internal debate I asked Mr. Ernest Maggs (who had the book in stock) to write me when he got another copy. On getting back to Farmington after I had turned the book over to Mr. Tinker on my return, I found a letter from Mr. Maggs saying that he thought I would be interested in a copy of *The Castle of Otranto* that had just come in—the copy Walpole gave to William Cole.

Cole, it turned out, had transcribed on its flyleaves some complimentary verses "To the Honourable and Ingenious Author" and the long passages that Walpole had written him about the composition of the book. "You will laugh at my earnestness," Walpole concluded, "but if I have amused you, by retracing with any fidelity the manners of ancient days, I am content, and give you leave to think me as idle as you please." That is Walpole's summing-up of his life's work. Posterity might think him frivolous and gossipy (it has thought him so), but that did not bother him much so long as posterity also believed that his history was accurate. If it did, he would gain the only immortality he believed in. Cole was an antiquary, and antiquaries are a link between the past and the future. Stating his purpose in life to Cole was stating it to the twentieth century. Walpole would have been pleased to know that Cole ran true to form in his copy of *The Castle of Otranto*.

2

Association items are usually spoken of by mature collectors with a certain condescension. The implication is that there is something soft and sentimental about them. Respect for "condition" and the desire to have one's books, if possible, as they first appeared are the second stage of the collector's progress. The

BENTLEY'S FRONTISPIECE TO HIS
DESIGNS FOR GRAY'S POEMS

collector is speeded to this stage if he is foolish enough to buy books described in booksellers' catalogues as "foxed," "loose in binding," "worn." A. W. Evans and Ned Streeter helped me see the beauties and utilities of condition. They agreed that an uncut copy of *Bentley's Designs for Gray's Poems* (Evans had one in stock) was a better book than Mrs. Vesey's trimmed copy of the same book (which I owned). The book from her library, with her name on a fly-leaf, had made me see Mrs. Vesey ("the Sylph" to her friends) fluttering about at one of her conversation parties, radiating goodness, ear-trumpet at the ready. Evans and Ned were embarrassed when I said this, for in the light of bibliography it was childish babble.

Bibliography was the new science recently opened up by A. W. Pollard, Sir Walter Greg, and R. B. McKerrow. R. W. Chapman was its chief exponent for eighteenth-century books. The word "bibliography" was (and is) confusing, because it is used to mean different things. A list of books on a subject is a bibliography of that subject; a list of an author's written work is a bibliography of that author. Early in the nineteenth century Dibdin used the word to mean book-collecting, and later Rive used it as a description of books "and other literary arrangements." But Pollard and his coadjutors when they talk of bibliography have in mind something more definite and complex. They are talking about the mechanics of book-production, the part played and the techniques used by compositor and pressman and "the relation of the text as it finally appears to the author's manuscript, especially dealing with the errors which may be introduced by the processes through which it has passed." "Each book," said McKerrow, "presents its own problems and has to be investigated by methods suited to its particular case. . . . With almost every book we take up we are in new country." Something of all this was communicated to me by Evans and Ned Streeter.

Eighteenth-century books were normally issued in paper boards or wrappers. Since eighteenth-century purchasers of new books usually sent them to a binder to be bound in calf or morocco, books in their original condition, which are called "pristine" or "mint," are what the bibliographer wants, since the binder in substituting calf or morocco for the original boards may have removed or destroyed various features of bibliographical interest. Whether he did so or not, in cutting down the book he certainly altered its appearance. Books in pristine state are of course much rarer than rebound books and so are more valuable. As bibliography developed in the twenties, the prices of books rose with the width of their margins; an extra millimeter might advance the cost of a book by pounds.

New facts were discovered every day in eighteenth-century books, not merely the teasing "points" of unscholarly collectors and booksellers, not just a dropped letter here, a misspelling there, but more important matters involving paper and watermarks, "cancels" (pages that have been suppressed during publication and rewritten), the rearrangement of the order and relative value of different editions of a book, and, finally and most excitingly, the discovery and demonstration of forgeries. The books printed by Walpole at the Strawberry Hill Press furnish an ideal opportunity for the practice and study of bibliography.

When Walpole founded the Press, in 1757, he had written a number of tracts and essays that had been well received. He was, in his fortieth year, ready to write something more ambitious, but he shrank from inviting the controversies that eighteenth-century publications inspired. "To make anything one writes . . . public, is giving everybody leave under one's own hand to call one fool," he said. A private press was a happy way out for him.

On the inside cover of his "Journal of the Printing Office at Strawberry Hill" below his name and the date, 1757, Walpole wrote: "Archbishop Parker kept in his house a Painter, Engraver, and Printer." Parker was a pioneer of English learning, the patron of the first private press in England, and the first great English bibliophile. Below this significant line Walpole pasted a cutting from the *Craftsman* of February 20, 1731 that described a press "set up at St. James's for the Royal Family to observe and enjoy the Noble Art of Printing." "We could wish," the *Craftsman* concludes, "that our Nobility and Gentry would follow this Royal Example, and set up a Printing Press in their Houses." Walpole was the first eighteenth-century man to do so.

The advantage of being your own author, editor, and printer (by proxy) is obvious; you write and print just what you please when and how you please; you give your books away to whom you please; you can even sell them through a friendly bookseller if you please. A privately printed book is above the strife, yet if you give a copy of it to a friendly critic he will probably publish a friendly review of it. All this was as true in the eighteenth century as it is today, but in the eighteenth century professional authorship was a "low" calling. "The mob of gentlemen who wrote with ease" did not, as a rule, grant their effusions public dispersal. It is significant that Walpole's first extended work was *A Catalogue of Royal and Noble Authors*: the example of these exalted persons should help to improve the status of a profession in which he wished to engage.

Apart from Gray's *Odes*, the autobiography of *Lord Herbert of Cherbury*, and Walpole's *Anecdotes of Painting in England*, the productions of the Press are not much read today, but everything that Walpole thought worth printing was given long reviews in the eighteenth-century magazines, and all—including the verses of his friends, the verses he wrote for his lady visitors when they inspected the Press, the title-pages he printed for his special collections—are of concern to a Walpole collector.

At first I bought only association copies of the Strawberry Hill Press books—Walpole's own copies of them or copies he gave to his friends. Later it became clear to me that a collection that hoped to be unrivaled must have copies in their original condition. Adding them gave me a good many duplicates, but among them were certain "variants." A variant is a book in which the pages have an accidental displacement of type or a correction of the text after the work was begun to be printed. A particularly puzzling variant in the Strawberry Hill Press books occurred in Gray's *Odes* (1757), "The Bard" and "Progress of Poesy," the first book printed at the Press. In 1929 it was pointed out that a few copies were printed on thick paper with two misprints, a puzzle that engaged some of the best bibliographical minds for years. Since I am not a bibliographer, I invited Allen T. Hazen to solve the puzzle and to discover and solve the other puzzles I felt sure the Press provided, for descriptive bibliographies of Walpole's works and of the Press were essential to an understanding of him. *A Bibliography of the Strawberry Hill Press* (1942) and *A Bibliography of Horace Walpole* (1948) were the result. These two works have been accepted as landmarks in the study of bibliography.

As soon as Hazen was embarked upon the *Bibliography of Strawberry Hill,* I was seized by an acute attack of bibliomania. The Folger Shakespeare Library is the shining example of the value of buying many copies of the same book. Mr. Folger bought seventy-seven copies of the First Folio, about half the known copies, to aid students of textual problems in Shakespeare. This is a much higher percentage of the whole than I aspired to, but ten per cent of the number of copies printed at the Strawberry Hill Press did not seem too fantastic a goal. In Walpole's Journal of the Press we have his word for the number of copies he printed of each book. There were 34 books (several are of only a few pages) and, in addition, 78 "Detached Pieces," which included title-pages, labels for books, and cards of address. The number of copies ran from 2,000 (Gray's *Odes*) to a single title-page.

THE PRINTING OFFICE

I failed to get ten per cent of the entire output of the Press, but I did get duplicates of most of the titles—in some cases more than twenty copies—which Allen Hazen was able to use for collation and comparison. Since many of them are presentation copies, they have a biographical as well as a bibliographical interest.

Collecting the publications of a private press is like filling a page in a stamp album: you are not so much concerned with the value of each individual item as you are with filling a gap. You care more for a book that is rare than for one that is common, no matter what the book may be. To a collector of the Strawberry Hill Press, Walpole's *Hieroglyphic Tales,* of which only 7 copies were printed, is a far more desirable book than Gray's *Odes,* of which 2,000 copies were printed.

There have been many collections of the Press from the eighteenth century to the present. Four of them I was able to buy almost *en bloc,* the Gaskill and Spoor collections in this country, the Geoffrey Madan and Waldegrave collections in England. Buying *en bloc* is not so satisfying a way to collect as buying each lot separately, but it has its advantages for a bibliographer who wants as much evidence as possible as soon as he can get it. My wholesale buying turned up unrecorded variants in nearly every book; it also helped Allen Hazen prove that Walpole's printer–secretary,

Thomas Kirgate, was a forger, among whose works manufactured out of wedlock was the thick-paper *Odes.*

Hazen's *Bibliography of Horace Walpole* includes Walpole's works, prefaces, and editorial contributions that were not printed at the Press. My final review of the book in proof was made, owing to a temporary inability to use my eyes, by the aid of my wife, who read the entire work aloud to me. I was struck then not only by the readability of it, but by the demonstration that such a bibliography is also a biography. *A Bibliography of Horace Walpole* is less dramatic than the earlier volume, for no forgeries were found, but the study threw a great deal of new light on Walpole's books and even added new titles to the Walpolian canon. *A Bibliography of Horace Walpole* is not without drama: Louis XVI corrected his translation of *The Historic Doubts of King Richard the Third* in the Tuileries while awaiting execution; a youth of seventeen, a member of the *Résistance* during the recent war, made a translation of *The Castle of Otranto.* This last was printed by his father, who, when he sent me a copy of it, said that his son had hoped to come to Farmington after the war to pursue his Walpolian studies. But that was not to be, for the boy was captured by the Germans and was never seen again.

The *Bibliography of Horace Walpole* also produced a dramatic moment at the thirtieth reunion of
my class at Yale. When two members of the class said
on the Sunday morning that they would like to see
the Yale Library, James T. Babb, the Librarian, very
kindly came down and opened it up for us. He was
standing at the main entrance holding a small book
in his hand when we, some eighty of us, trooped in.
Carried away by the sight of so many of my classmates
who had chosen to visit the library instead of the local golf courses, I spoke for a few minutes on the
glories of the place and concluded with as handsome
a bouquet as I could fabricate at the moment for Jim
Babb. The *Bibliography of Horace Walpole,* he then
explained, was just out. In it was described a book
that had not hitherto been known to be by Walpole.
Only seven copies of the work were mentioned; none
of them was at Farmington. On the other hand, three
of the seven were in the Yale Library, or rather, he
should say, only two were there because—and he
handed the book he was holding to me—he and the
staff of the library now gave me Yale's third copy
"with our appreciation and affection."

To me the most absorbing passages in these bibliographies are those that give the "provenance," or
histories of individual copies. "Provenance," Harvey
Cushing once said to me, "is the tertiary phase of bib-

liomania." One does not have to know what a forme is or understand the mysteries of imposition to taste its joys. To know that your copy of a book was formerly in a famous library, to know when and for how much it was sold, who bought it, and what then became of it, step by step, until it reached your own shelf, to recognize the marks of ownership of these former owners, perhaps to find the lot numbers of the various auction sales through which the book has passed, this is the ultimate satisfaction to a collector. "Such well-attested descent," wrote Horace Walpole, "is the genealogy of the objects of virtù—not so noble as those of the peerage, but on a par with those of race-horses. In all three, especially the pedigrees of peers and rarities, the line is often continued by many insignificant names."

I have a book that passes in review the three stages of the collector's journey, the stages marked by partiality to association copies, condition, and provenance. It is a copy of Walpole's *Hieroglyphic Tales* (1785), one of the seven copies that he printed at his press. Although I had the original manuscript, I did not own a printed copy of it until recently. Three of the seven copies are in public institutions; three have disappeared. I knew where the seventh was and after waiting twenty years I got it. This is the copy Walpole bequeathed to Thomas Barrett, the man he saw carrying on the Gothic tradition into the nineteenth century. It is thus an association item, and its condition is such, after one hundred and sixty-five years, as must be seen to be believed: it is uncut, in the original wrappers, and as fresh as it was on the day it came from the Press, for it has been preserved in the wrapping-paper in which it was then placed and on which Walpole wrote: "A Strawberry Edition to be delivered on my death to Thomas Barrett, Esq. of Lee, in Kent." Finally, nearly all of its subsequent history down to the other day is known from its appearance at Sotheby's, July 12, 1859, in the sale of Barrett's library, lot 513, when it was sold to Boone, the dealer, for five guineas. One of the missing links was the place where its late owner bought it. This was supplied by John Carter, of Scribner's, who, when he saw the book, recognized the Scribner price in code inside the front cover and kindly translated it for me.

VII

I

IF I COULD keep only one book it would be the scrap-book into which Walpole pasted Richard Bentley's drawings for the remodeling of Strawberry Hill. The whole Walpolian structure rests upon this book, for Strawberry Hill is a projection of Horace Walpole himself.

Walpole rented the cottage that was to become his "castle" in 1747, in his thirtieth year. "The house is so small," he wrote, "that I can send it you in a letter to look at: the prospect is as delightful as possible, commanding the river, the town, and Richmond Park; and being situated on a hill descends to the Thames through two or three little meadows, where I have some Turkish sheep and cows, all studied in their colors for becoming the view." Two years later he purchased the property and began to plan the al-terations that were to make Strawberry Hill famous throughout Europe.

He decided to remodel his cottage in the Gothic style. To help him with this imaginative and tricky project he formed what he called the Committee on Taste, composed of himself, John Chute, an older virtuoso whom he had met in Florence, and Richard Bentley, the son of the great Master of Trinity. Walpole supplied the money and an instinct for scholarly research. He also supplied the enthusiasm. "Gothic" had become in his mind a symbol of England's antiquity and greatness. England had as fine buildings and as venerable as any he had seen on the Grand Tour. Why shouldn't Englishmen be proud of their country's arts? England, which had just emerged from the inconclusive War of the Austrian Succession as a formidable European power, was going through a phase of national self-consciousness similar to that of this country's in 1920, when we built houses and public buildings in the Colonial style and filled them with Colonial furniture, much of it necessarily from Grand Rapids. Just as we discovered our past, so Walpole and his friends carried forward the "Gothic movement."

The committee went about its work conscientiously. There were abroad other neo-Goths who did not understand what they were doing, who were, in fact, little better than charlatans; their "bad attempts in Gothic" must be avoided and could be avoided by research. "Gothic" meant not merely visions and patriotism, but study. So the committee went back to the original buildings or prints of them. Familiarity with the great topographical works—Dart and Dugdale chief among them—was essential to success. The results of all this research are set forth in the *Description of Strawberry Hill*, which Walpole later printed at his press. The ceiling of the Gallery, for example, was "taken from one of the side aisles of Henry VII's Chapel" in Westminster Abbey, the chimneypiece in the Holbein Chamber was "chiefly taken from the tomb of Archbishop Warham at Canterbury," as shown in Dart's *Canterbury* at page 480. The committee saw no impropriety in converting a tomb to a chimneypiece or in substituting wood for stone: were they not copying Gothic from the masters? Stresses and strains they wisely left to a professional builder who knew how to build towers and battlements in plaster, which, although they wore out rapidly, did not fall down. (Long before his death, it was said that "Mr. Walpole has already outlived three sets of his battlements.") Walpole pasted Bentley's designs in a folio scrapbook and printed a special title-page for it.

Bentley's drawings have upon them evidences of the committee's differences of opinion; Chute has drawn a line here, Walpole made a note there. Bentley scribbled the measurements and directions to the builder on the side. "For the library," Walpole wrote

BENTLEY'S REJECTED DRAWING FOR THE LIBRARY

Bentley of his design, "it cannot have the Strawberry imprimatur: the double arches and double pinnacles are most ungraceful; and the doors below the bookcases in Mr. Chute's designs had a conventual look, which yours totally wants." Bentley had other failures. A Chinese building for the garden and a columbarium for the house were given a great deal of thought, but abandoned, as were several other projects intended for the houses and gardens of Walpole's friends. Yet though much was discarded, much was created. The Gateway and North Entrance of Strawberry, the Entrance Hall, and Staircase, the Holbein Chamber, the chimneypiece in the Little Parlour, Refectory, the Blue, Yellow, and Red Bedchambers, the Shell Bench, the Gothic Lanthorn; all these are to be found in Bentley's book of *Designs,* and all were executed to the wonder and delight of the eighteenth century. Elsewhere in the book are Bentley's preliminary sketches for Gray's poems, including his unpublished illustrations for "The Bard," and flights of his own fancy, among them a Temptation of St. Anthony.

Bentley's book is one of the springs of the Romantic movement. The committee's intention was to set Strawberry whispering from its towers the last enchantments of the Middle Ages. How this was to be managed was made clear by the intimate friend of the committee Thomas Gray:

To raise the ceiling's fretted height,
Each panel in achievements clothing,
Rich windows that exclude the light
And passages that lead to nothing.

Strawberry Hill is one of the most influential houses ever built. Its descendants are to be found in every dominion in the Empire and in every state in the Union. The Old Library at Yale is one; the Governor's House at Sydney is another. "This book," said Evans when I took it to Cork Street for him to see, "is a landmark in English taste." While we were talking, Dr. Rosenbach came into the shop. He turned a few pages of the book and then gave it a great slap. "That's the finest Walpole item in the world!" he shouted, and I think he was right, as usual.

I bought the book indirectly from X shortly before the English general strike in May 1926, which, ignobly and wisely, I avoided by going to Paris, leaving the awkward folio behind. In Paris I fretted about it; when would I see it again? I had it flown across the Channel, and it thus became, probably, the first (but not the last) unique Walpole item to leave the country of its origin by air. It was well that I had the drawings in Paris, for I showed them to Seymour de Ricci, the most learned bibliophile of the day. Bentley's drawings set his fabulous memory working, and in a few days he turned up still other drawings of Strawberry Hill by Bentley that had formerly been in my book. These he insisted upon my taking at the price he paid for them years before, although it was only, as I told him, one hundredth of what I had paid X. Later I was to get the originals of Bentley's celebrated *Designs for Six Poems by Mr. T. Gray,* a book that is also a landmark in its way and that inspired Gray to write his "Stanzas to Mr. Bentley," in which he compares his lyre unfavorably with Bentley's pencil:

> See in their course, each transitory thought
> Fix'd by his touch a lasting essence take;
> Each dream, in Fancy's airy colouring wrought
> To local symmetry and life awake!

Later still I got Chute's designs for Strawberry Hill, which prove that he played a much greater part in its creation than had been supposed; but, as I have said, if I could keep only one book in my entire collection, it would be Bentley's *Designs for Strawberry Hill.*

The first account that Walpole printed of any part of his house was a *Catalogue of Pictures and Drawings in the Holbein Chamber* (1760). In a prefatory note Walpole explained that the pictures marked "thus* . . . were taken off on oil-paper by Mr.

Vertue from the original drawings of Holbein, in Queen Caroline's closet at Kensington.

"The ceiling was drawn by Mr. Müntz from the Queen's dressing-room at Windsor.

"The screen was designed by Mr. Bentley: the pierced arches are taken from the gate of the choir at Rouen.

"The mosaic of the windows was painted, and the whole put together by Mr. Price of Hatton Garden."

Walpole continued throughout his life recording the Additions and More Additions to Strawberry Hill. These he tacked on to his *Description of the Villa of Horace Walpole, Youngest Son of Sir Robert Walpole Earl of Orford, at Strawberry Hill near Twickenham. With an Inventory of the Furniture, Pictures, Curiosities, etc.,* which he first printed in 1774 in an edition of one hundred copies. In 1784 he printed two hundred copies of an enlarged edition with prints. At the moment I have thirty-six copies of these two editions. There is something special about nearly every one. Seven, for example, Walpole left as bequests to friends. Other copies have variants; still others belonged to Walpole's printer-secretary, Thomas Kirgate, who extra-illustrated and sold them after Walpole's death. The most rewarding copies of all are, of course, the four copies annotated by Walpole himself.

View in the flower Garden.

THE GARDEN AT STRAWBERRY HILL

I got the first of them in 1927. It is inlaid in a vast
folio with Walpole's arms on the sides. In it Walpole
pasted the water-color drawings he commissioned the
best topographical artists of the day to make of Strawberry. These drawings by Edward Edwards, Paul
Sandby, John Carter, J. C. Barrow, and William Pars
show, which the prints of them do not, that Strawberry did cast a spell. The views of the interiors con-
vey the air of mystery and "gloomth" for which the
Committee on Taste strove. The outdoor views make
it clear that Strawberry was a pleasant place, with
lawns and trees and borders. The light of late summer filters down between the beeches and elms.
Perhaps Kirgate is shown carrying a portfolio of
prints as he leaves the cottage in the garden; perhaps
two or three gardeners with rakes and a barrow are
tidying up the lawn before the Great Cloister; perhaps we are looking toward the East Front while a
distant coach lumbers along the road to Twickenham.
Perhaps, again, the September clouds are reflected
in the pool, Po-yang, from which the heron stole the
goldfish. The opening of the high wall to the west is
flanked by hollyhocks; through it we catch a glimpse
of poplars and another verdurous vista. A gardener
slopes along, watering-can in hand. Across the pool,
Walpole himself strolls with a lady on his arm. Who
is she? Lady Browne? Lady Herries? Lady Cecilia

Johnston? In his left hand Walpole has a cane, which at the moment he is pointing in the direction of the Great Tower. "Could I describe the gay but tranquil scene where [Strawberry] stands, and add the beauty of the landscape to the romantic cast of the mansion, it would raise more pleasing sensations than a dry list of curiosities can excite," he wrote in his Preface to the *Description*; "at least the prospect would recall the good humour of those who might be disposed to condemn the fantastic fabric, and to think it a very proper habitation of, as it was the scene that inspired, the author of *The Castle of Otranto*." Something of this he may be saying to his companion by the pool in the flower garden. Having said it, he restores the cane to its proper function and hobbles on, the lady delightedly attending, through the garden and into the house.

2

My first visit to Strawberry took place in April 1925. Two American friends and I went in a taxi to Twickenham, rang the doorbell, and talked ourselves in, a crass piece of intrusion. Strawberry had recently come under the direction of the Congregation of St. Vincent de Paul, which was soon to open there a training college (St. Mary's) for teachers. As the Fathers had not yet taken up residence, it was not open to the public, but an army with banners is not more terrible than a collector who wants to see something.

Strawberry has suffered little by alteration, but the few changes are confusing to one who has puzzled for years over its eighteenth-century appearance. The first impression that the visitor has today is of smallness: the earliest rooms do strike one as being tiny. After repeated visits this impression changes, for by American and modern standards the house is really very large. Gradually one is able to enter into the spirit of the place and to feel what Walpole wanted visitors to feel, "the romantic cast of the mansion." The ridicule that has been heaped upon Strawberry Hill perhaps stimulates a defense of it. At any rate, I find it much more attractive than twentieth-century "Collegiate Gothic," perhaps because its dignified Georgian frame is so conspicuous. In Strawberry Hill you see the Romantic movement in the very act of rising out of the Augustan Age. Strawberry's pastiche is pioneer and amateurish, not professional and stale. When the Committee on Taste pointed its doors and windows and excluded the light with windows richly dight, their "Gothic" did not go all through the building; it remained on the surface, where they placed it with a certain gaiety. "In truth," wrote Walpole, "I did not mean to make my house so Gothic as to exclude convenience and modern refinements in luxury. . . . It was built to please my own taste and in some degree to realize my own visions." It was "a plaything house," he said. As such, to one twentieth-century visitor at least, it is completely successful.

My second and subsequent visits to Strawberry Hill were conducted in an orderly manner, by means of a proper introduction from Lady Lavery to the Vice-Principal, Father J. Leonard, the editor of St. Vincent's letters. My wife and I found that he had not only a just appreciation of Horace Walpole, but a deep and affectionate interest in everything American. We doubled his American acquaintance, our predecessors having been Lady Lavery and Henry James. He later supplemented his American studies by making a trip across the Atlantic, a regrettably short one, for his stay in the United States was limited to six days, of which he had barely one for Farmington.

On my first authorized visit to Strawberry Hill, Father Leonard pointed to a tiny fragment of molding on the mantel of the fireplace in the Red Bedchamber. It was a bit of the original molding, he told us. "I am now going out of the room," he said, and went.

I looked at my wife. The intention was clear. "What do you think?" I asked.

STRAWBERRY HILL TODAY

"Oh, no!"

We stood transfixed by moral rectitude. Father
Leonard returned and saw the molding untouched.

"The New England conscience, is it? Now I am
going out again." When he returned the second time,
the molding had disappeared. It has been followed to
Farmington by other bits and pieces of Strawberry
that Father Leonard sent over in the thirties: a strip
of the painted ceiling in the library, a window from
the Great Bedchamber. It would have been much
simpler and cheaper for the college to have torn
down the house and started afresh, yet regard for its
place in the history of English architecture has moved
the college to keep as much of the original fabric as
possible. London has reached and passed Strawberry's
gates, suburban villas cut off its views of the Thames
and curtail the sweep of its lawns, but now that the
damage caused by two German incendiary bombs has
been repaired, the lover of the eighteenth century
may again visit the toy castle on which the England
of George III could discern, in the words of Strawberry Hill's creator, "the true rust of the Barons'
Wars."

VIII

I

IN THE Beverly Chew Sale of December 1924, which, the reader may recall, was the moment of decision for me, there was, besides Walpole's copy of Gray's *Odes,* his annotated set of Pope, 1743–51, in seven volumes. The first sight of one of those pages crowded with Walpole's neat and legible hand worked powerfully on my imagination. When opposite the line:

The Priest whose Flattery be-dropt the Crown,

Walpole wrote: "Dr. Gilbert, afterwards Archbishop of York, affected to cry in the pulpit, preaching on the death of the Queen," it was the portrait gallery again, with the subjects stepping down out of their frames.

The more I thought about Walpole's set of Pope, the more I wanted it. I had taken the plunge at Scribner's; if I was to have the finest collection of Horace Walpole in the world, I mustn't begin by losing Walpole's set of Pope. Unfortunately, I went down to the sale and sat, in a state of agitation, with

Byrne Hackett of the Brick Row, who bid for me. Although my limit seemed high to us, the bidding went higher, much higher, right up out of sight. Hackett finally got it in the stratosphere. The under-bidder was Lingle of the George D. Smith Company. Months later when I asked Lingle why he had bid on the book, he said that when he saw how much I wanted it he assumed that others would want it, too. Although the lot went for seven and a half times what it had fetched in 1901, Hackett soon sold it for twice what he paid for it, or fifteen times the 1901 price. When it reached my shelves, fifteen years after the Chew Sale, it came at a considerable discount, but still at ten times the 1901 figure. I tell this, not only to mention the first book I ever saw from Walpole's library, but to illustrate the vagaries of the auction room and the irresponsibility of collectors.

The lesson I learned at the Chew Sale has saved me money. The lesson is: don't go to auctions. The lesson was repeated to me by X. I have forgotten it only once, at the Spoor Sale at the Parke-Bernet, in 1939. The Spoor library had one of the most important Walpole collections ever sold in this country. There were about twenty items in it that I wanted, and I couldn't stay away. Tinker went down to New York to keep me company in that fateful hour. We sat with Hackett, who had my bids and who did extremely well for me until Sheridan's annotated copy of Walpole's *Mysterious Mother* came up. Whereas the other lots had fallen to us without a struggle, this lot was contested. It went stubbornly up and then paused. Arthur Swann, the auctioneer, who has been a good friend of my library, looked in our direction. In a panic I thought we were going to lose the book unless immediate action was taken. I waved my hand wildly, and the book was knocked down to me. Then I discovered that I was also the underbidder, for when I waved my hand the bid was Hackett's.

The second book from Strawberry Hill that I saw was Lord Baltimore's *Cœlestes et Inferi* (Venice, 1771), a book as rare as it is unimportant. It was at Scribner's on the day in December 1924 when I made my first purchases there. It has a note in Walpole's hand. I did not get it until 1938, when it was sold at Sotheby's for one twelfth the Scribner price in 1924. I saw my third book from Walpole's library shortly after my first Scribner visit: when Gabriel Wells produced a volume containing four poems that Walpole had bound with his arms on the sides and "Poems of Geo. 3" on the spine, I promptly bought it.

Since then I have had a chance to buy about eight hundred volumes from Walpole's library and have acquired all but four of them. The absence of these four I bitterly regret; the failure to buy one of them, in particular, is my biggest mistake as a collector. The book was a manuscript copy of *Ædes Walpolianæ* in folio, extra-illustrated by Walpole with many prints and drawings. The book was sent me on approval in 1925; the price was not high, considering what the book is. There were extenuating circumstances that help to explain my failure to buy it, but they are small comfort to me now: I had spent every available penny I had in England, and my ignorance at that time kept me from recognizing the text as being in Walpole's youthful hand. I told W. M. Ivins, Jr., then the curator of prints at the Metropolitan Museum, about the book, and he, of course, moved promptly. It is now in the Metropolitan and, such is bibliomania, that I still feel, after twenty-five years, that a part of me is lying on a shelf in the museum's Print Room.

2

Seymour de Ricci has this to say in his *English Collectors of Books and Manuscripts, 1530–1930:* "Although the library of Horace Walpole . . . contained some very valuable books and manuscripts, the interest attached to it was on the whole more sentimental than strictly bibliographical." Two years after publishing this, de Ricci spent the summer helping me discover the whereabouts of letters to and from Walpole. "What did I say about his library in my book?" he asked one day, and when I couldn't tell him, he treated himself to that elixir of the scholar, a rereading of his own work. He read it aloud and then added: "That is not nearly good enough." Another judgment of Horace Walpole had been revised.

When one first turns over the pages of the Strawberry Hill Sale Catalogue, one can hardly fail to agree with de Ricci's original verdict if one judges Walpole's library by "strictly bibliographical" values. De Ricci's comment is a rather dressy way of saying that Walpole did not own many books that would have reached four figures in a New York sale room during the twenties. Walpole owned one or two fine Books of Hours, Tottel's *Miscellany* (1557), Gosson's *School of Abuse* (1579), but they should be regarded as happy accidents; he did not collect books as he collected coins, medals, and engraved English portraits. What, then, did de Ricci mean when he said that his pronouncement upon Walpole's library was "not nearly good enough"?

There were about 7,500 volumes at Strawberry Hill, which was not a large total for an eighteenth-century country-house library. They were distributed through three rooms, of which the most interesting was the library Walpole built in 1754. It was 28 feet long, 17 feet wide, and 15 feet high, and it had shelves

THE LIBRARY

entirely around the walls, except for the chimney and one window that looked upon the Thames. The library had three features that gave its owner particular satisfaction. One of these was the ceiling painted by Clermont from Walpole's design. It displayed the shield of Walpole surrounded with the quarters borne by the family and heraldic embellishments. "At the four corners," Walpole wrote, "are shields, helmets, and mantles; on one shield is a large H, on another a W, semée of cross crosslets." The chimney-piece, he recorded, was "imitated from the tomb of John of Eltham, earl of Cornwall, in Westminster Abbey," but what the Committee on Taste had really done was to copy the print of it in Dart's *Westminster*. The "doors" to the bookcases supplied the third special feature of the room. They were "Gothic arches of pierced work" that swung on hinges before each section of books and were "taken from a side door case to the choir in Dugdale's *St. Paul's*." Thus were the ages of romance brought into the library. Little furniture was brought with them. There were a Louis Quatorze writing-table, six ebony chairs, five screens, an osprey modeled in terra cotta by Mrs. Damer, seven ossuaria, and a clock, a present from Henry VIII to Anne Boleyn. Eighteenth-century rooms were not comfortable by present-day standards.

Each bookcase was assigned a letter, beginning

with A to the right of the fireplace and extending around the room to M on the left of the fireplace. Between D and E was the "Glass Closet" in which Walpole kept under lock and key the books and manuscripts he particularly valued or did not wish everyone to see. The Glass Closet was originally a door that opened upon the Armoury, but proved to be a convenient way of adding another section to the library when the need for more shelves became imperative. Here were prudently placed the very few books in the library that would come under the modern rubric "erotica," and certain contemporary books in which Walpole had written notes of a personal nature. Among the manuscripts were several volumes from Sir Julius Cæsar's library and Mme du Deffand's letters and notebooks that she bequeathed to Walpole.

In 1763 Walpole notes he had plenty of room for growth, but the library filled up rapidly. His secretary-printer, Thomas Kirgate, wrestled with the shelves in A and B. "Those books that were on the third shelf in A," Kirgate notes, "are carried to the sixth; those on the fifth to the seventh and so upward. Those on the fifth in B are carried to the sixth and the others upward." Brave but unavailing struggle! All collectors and librarians know these growing-pains; Walpole was fortunate in being able to provide the only satisfactory solution, an additional room. In fact, he added not one room but two, both completed in 1790. The larger of these was on the upper floor of the new "Offices," the smaller was a room in the Round Tower fitted up for the books of prints originally in cases (or presses) B, C, and D. There was a fourth library, as a matter of fact, a mysterious one built in 1765, in what Walpole called "The Cottage in the Flower Garden." In his *Description of Strawberry Hill* he speaks of "several volumes of manuscripts" being in this library and states that there was "over the bookcases, a small marble bust of Lord Chancellor Clarendon," but he does not say what printed books were on the shelves. Whatever they were, Mrs. Damer records in her copy of the *Description* that when she moved into Strawberry, on Walpole's death, she found them worm-eaten and spoiling with damp and neglect and removed them to the library in the Offices.

We can speak with confidence of the rest of the books because of the Manuscript Catalogue Walpole had made of the library in 1763 and the two Sale Catalogues of 1842. The Manuscript Catalogue was written in a professional hand, presumably by someone from Walpole's office at the Exchequer. Walpole kept it up himself for a few years after 1763. Thereafter it was neglected, probably until the mid-nineties when Kirgate added a few more entries; in other words, the Manuscript Catalogue does not show many of the books bought after 1766. These are supplied by the Sale Catalogue of 1842. Finally, the recovery of three quarters of the bound volumes of tracts, plays, and poems gives us the titles of their otherwise unidentified contents.

The arrangement of the books was not in accord with modern library practice. The method employed was what I believe is now called "fixed location." Above the bookplate in each book in the main library was written a shelf-mark, unless the end-paper was marbled, in which case the shelf-mark was written on the following white paper. The shelf-mark consisted of the letter of the case, the number of the shelf counting from the floor, and the position of the book on the shelf from the left. Thus H.6.9. was in Case H, on the sixth shelf, the ninth book on the shelf from the left. The books in the Round Tower and the Offices had only a letter, A through Y, to indicate the case, and one digit to indicate the shelf, for by the time those libraries were arranged Walpole and Kirgate had discovered that it was useless to try to keep the books in their proper places on the shelves.

It seems likely that Walpole directed the original arrangement in a casual way. Case A contained a preponderance of biography and books by noble authors;

B, books on the arts and numismatics; C and D, books of prints and drawings; E, topography; F and G, French literature; H, I, and K, English literature; and L and M, the classics; but even so settled and stable a case as K had a lot in the Sale Catalogue made up of "Revolution at Naples by Massaniello, the Art of Curing by Expectation, King William the Third's Letters and Diary, 2 vols; Howell's Dodona's Grove, English Grammar, and Tosi on Singers."

It took me more than six years to piece out the account of the library that I have given here. First I noticed the shelf-marks in the books I got from Walpole's library; then I noticed that the letters on them usually corresponded with the case in which they had been sold in 1842 (E.8.19. was sold with the books in Case E). The discovery of the Manuscript Catalogue at Lord Walpole's (through the introduction of Wyndham Ketton-Cremer) made the arrangement of the books perfectly clear. Finally, a subsequent visit to Strawberry Hill showed the cases themselves with their letters still plainly painted on "the Gothic arches of pierced work" before each case.

3

The 1842 sale led off with the dispersal of the books in Cases A, B, and C. It had been planned to sell the library in the first eight days, but there was so much dissatisfaction with the cataloguing of the prints and books of prints in the seventh and eighth days' sales (the contents of the library in the Round Tower) that these were removed, recatalogued, and sold in a ten-day sale at London the following June. Thus the sale of the library was made in two portions, which occupied sixteen days. There are six different issues of the Strawberry Hill Catalogue, of which the sixth issue is the all-important one, since it alone mentions most of the books. The sixth issue is easily recognized, for the additional books are printed in blacker type than the rest, and the seventh and eighth days' sales are omitted altogether.

In contrast to the crowds that visited Strawberry before the sale, at the sale itself there were few, other than the great dealers who, one unfriendly newspaper account asserted, were buying largely on commission. That this was not true of the booksellers is proved by the many books that appeared in their catalogues after the sale, some of which, those issued by Thorpe, Payne and Foss, and Strong of Bristol, were largely filled with books from Strawberry Hill; but it is true that nearly all of the leading collectors wanted at least one volume from the library and that few bid themselves. Several collectors bought dozens of books: Beckford bought through Bohn; Lord Derby through Boone. The books acquired by Henry Labouchère were bought at the sale by Thorpe, Payne and Foss, and Bohn, and it would seem that he bought his books from their stocks. John Britton's extensive purchases came from Strong, who worked closely with Thorpe in what was perhaps an early version of the "knock-out." A few private collectors had the temerity to buy in person: Richard Bentley and Henry Colburn were two of them; Sir Thomas Phillipps was another; Ralph Sneyd was still another. The prices were not considered brilliant; the only author to bring consistently high prices was Horace Walpole himself. The total realized for the books, prints, and books of drawings was £3,837.15.6. Heaven knows what that represents now, or what the library would fetch today; I have bought two or three of the books for less than their 1842 price, but the average cost to me has been nearer six times those figures.

Lord Derby's purchases at Knowsley and those of the British Museum are the only ones, so far as I know, that are in the library for which they were bought. The rest have wandered far and wide. About eight hundred volumes, as I have said, are at Farmington. Surprisingly few of the books have found their way into public libraries. Of these the three chief repositories are the British Museum, with about one hundred and fifty volumes (of which half formed two lots at the sale), Harvard, and the Victoria and

Albert, which have about thirty-five volumes apiece. "New" books turn up all the time. During the twenty-six years I have been reassembling Walpole's library, I have acquired a *title* from it on the average of one every four and a half days—a title, not a volume. (The bound volumes of tracts, plays, and poems average about ten titles to a volume; I have about 150 of these volumes, of which 110 were bought from the estate of Sir Leicester Harmsworth.) In all, about a third of the titles in the original library may be examined today. That this is the most interesting third of the library, both from the bibliographical and from the Walpolian standpoint, would seem to be likely: good books have higher powers of survival than inferior books; Walpole's notes in his copies have acted as a preservative in those copies he annotated.

What proportion of the original library survives I have no idea. Many of Walpole's books have been destroyed, not by fire or flood, but by the trade. I have been told by old-time booksellers that before there was a market for any book from Walpole's library, they thought little of pulping unimportant books formerly in it that were in poor condition. The bookplate was always worth half a crown. The dealers soaked it off and either sold it separately or pasted it into another book. They stripped off the covers and threw the book into a sack, which they sold for half a sovereign when it was filled. The covers, with the precious shelf-marks, went into the office fire. And so the book was literally destroyed. How many books were thus disposed of there is no way of knowing, but Walpole's bookplate is distressingly common.

The practice of pasting Walpole's bookplate into books that did not belong to him has supplied the market with a number of ghosts, some of which haunt the most august shelves. The presence of the bookplate brings conviction of authenticity to its owner, who goes on presenting the book as from Horace Walpole's library. Since all the books in the library had shelf-marks except the books in the Glass Closet, and all of those I have seen have Walpole's notes in them, the absence of the shelf-marks or Walpole's notes in a book with an eighteenth-century or earlier binding is suspicious. When, in addition, the Manuscript and Sale Catalogues show that Walpole did not own a copy of the book, the impostor stands revealed beyond any reasonable doubt.

A more difficult problem is to identify the books that really were Walpole's, but which are masquerading as ghosts. These are the books that were re-bound after the sale by their owners. The original covers with their shelf-marks are gone, and if there are no manuscript notes, the catalogue is the chief source of reassurance. Proof of Walpole's ownership may be supplied by the small marginalia he frequently made. These were short horizontal lines, crosses, and exclamation points in pencil.

Further evidence is furnished by the bookplate itself. Walpole had four bookplates. Two of these were made before he became Earl of Orford, two afterwards. In the second state, which was designed about 1766, Walpole's name is engraved in an elaborate script. By that time his taste in book-buying had changed somewhat; from then on he bought contemporary books much more frequently than older ones. Therefore a bookplate of the second state in a book printed before 1760 is suspicious unless it has other signs of Walpole's ownership. Finally, when later owners have disliked the marks of former owners, they have occasionally tried to erase Walpole's shelf-marks, sometimes with great but unavailing skill, for the paper is inevitably roughened and the erasers may have failed to remove the offset of the shelf-marks that frequently appears on the opposite flyleaf. (Whoever wrote the shelf-marks in the books —he was the same man who made the Manuscript Catalogue—was evidently in a hurry and shut the books before the ink was dry.) A more effective blotting-out was accomplished by new end-papers; Henry Gibbs, Lord Aldenham, used this method.

WALPOLE'S COPY OF *LADY MARY
WORTLEY MONTAGU'S LETTERS*

One of the Walpole books in his sale showed no shelf-marks, but, fortunately, Mr. Ernest Maggs bought it for me anyway. The end-papers were certainly nineteenth-century. I took the book down to the Yale Library to have the end-paper on the front cover removed. "I think," I said to the binder, "that you will find C.2.15 written in ink just about here," and so he did.

4

What use, it may now be asked, did Walpole make of his library? It is evident to any reader of his works and letters that he made constant use of it. *The Catalogue of Royal and Noble Authors* could not have been written without the books in Case A; *The Castle of Otranto*, Walpole himself said, was natural "for a head filled like mine with Gothic story." The Road to Otranto would be a comparatively easy one to follow.

Its starting-point goes far back into Walpole's life. At the age of seven he wrote to his "Dear Mamy" for Banks's *Earl of Essex* and Rowe's *Jane Shore*. We know that he was buying books when he was aged ten, doubtless from Pote of Eton. In his youth he wrote his name in his books and the year when he bought them on a flyleaf, a practice he unfortunately did not continue regularly. The books he bought while at Eton prove his statement that he "was never quite a schoolboy." In addition to his textbooks—Webster's *Practical Mathematics*, Palairet's *French Grammar*, Moll's *Maps of the Ancient World*—he bought and read the contemporary writers, Addison and Steele, Congreve, Prior, and Gay. The classical books he had at Eton included not only Virgil, Horace, and Ovid, but Petronius as well. His lifelong habit of annotating his books began at school; on a flyleaf of Moll's *Maps,* following his note linking Leonidas with Thermopylæ and Themistocles with Salamis, he wrote a graceful quatrain in French on Tasso.

Books that he particularly liked—topographical books and biographies—he would occasionally annotate so fully that he would exhaust the flyleaves and write on extra sheets that he then bound into the volume, and these notes frequently passed through the creative process and reappeared in his letters. Such interpolations were usually anecdotal and biographical; they were "ana," to use the eighteenth-century word. Walpole's annotated books became, in effect, commonplace books upon which he drew for his letters.

The library was primarily a "working" library, not a sentimental one. The books that Walpole collected were the tracts, plays, and poems that he brought together to assist him in writing the history of his time. A catalogue of the books at Strawberry Hill would be a biography of Horace Walpole. Such a catalogue has been in course of preparation for many years. Allen Hazen is now finishing it. This catalogue will show virtually all the titles in the library. Fortunately, the Manuscript Catalogue has the shelf-marks and the years when the books were published and so ensures an accuracy of identification that the Sale Catalogue rarely affords. What appears in the Sale Catalogue merely as *History of Virginia* becomes in the Manuscript Catalogue "Beverly's *History of Virginia,* 1722, H.4.25." We shall be able to show something of the migration of the books about the house; we may even be able to throw light on the malaise evident in Case B, which suffered an unexplained incursion from Case D. We shall be able to name a good many of the other owners of the copies before and after Walpole—the aspect of the library that appealed most strongly to Seymour de Ricci and made him realize that for the descriptive bibliographer Walpole's library is extraordinarily rich. We shall give the manuscript notes in the copies we have seen when they are of interest. And, finally, we shall try to show how Walpole used his books in writing his works and letters.

Then will emerge, I believe, a clearer view of the ambitious, long-suffering, far-sighted, and witty man who made the library. We can be certain, I think, that in every generation there will be some who will study it with pleasure.

IX

I

One morning in March 1925 I walked into the shop of Pickering & Chatto in King Street, St. James's. "I collect Horace Walpole," I explained, and added, trying to be modest about it, that I had "most of the usual things." Modesty was in order for one who had collected Walpole for just four months.

The man I was addressing seemed to me then to be rather elderly; I suppose he was almost sixty. He was short, with a generous gray mustache and a friendly interest in his customers that filtered to them rather than knocked them down. We Americans are used to salesmen who blaze away with all their batteries of charm firing on sight, and we have to adjust ourselves to the quieter technique of the English. Mr. Charles Massey was an example of the old-time bookseller, one of the best of them, as I was to discover.

"We have," he said, "several plays from Walpole's library," and then, when he saw the effect of his words, he called out: "Dudley, Watson! Fetch up one or two of the Walpole plays."

The first of the young men summoned, I later

133

learned, was his son; the second was the assistant who has spent virtually all of his life with the firm. Although Pickering & Chatto was (and is) one of the leading West End booksellers, the invoices have been for thirty years copied out in Watson's copperplate hand. Dudley and Watson sat at small tables in the rear of the long room, their faces to the wall, their backs to the light, in accordance with the discipline that required junior clerks to be as inconspicuous and uncomfortable as possible, yet ready for instant action.

It would take some time, Mr. Massey explained to me, "to look out" all the plays. Would I come back in a week's time? When I went back, there were 130 plays formerly Walpole's on a long mahogany table in the middle of the shop. I sat in a Chippendale armchair beside it. Mr. Massey stood at my left. The last public appearance of the collection was at Sotheby's in June 1914, he recalled. It was a large collection; there were hundreds of plays in it. They had been bound in calf by Walpole, but had been unbound by Messrs. Maggs, who had been the purchasers in 1914. "Dudley, Watson!" Mr. Massey called out. "Fetch up some of the Walpole bindings."

The tattered bindings that had contained the plays appeared, their spines hanging like battle flags. After the collection was sold in 1914, Maggs had ripped

VOLUME 58 OF "THEATRE OF GEO. 3"

out the Sheridan and Goldsmith, which they sold separately. (No one wanted the whole collection, either for itself or for Walpole.) The balance, some 550 plays, together with the bindings, they sold to Pickering & Chatto, who had been selling them off slowly for eleven years. The unsold plays were in the cellar, arranged under the authors' names. Since there were several copies of many of the plays, Dudley and Watson were only certain that a copy had been Walpole's when they found in it a note in his hand. These notes were usually merely "November" or "February," written under the date on the title-page. The copies that had proof of his ownership they brought upstairs and laid on the table.

The bindings were of particular interest. Walpole wrote on the inside cover of each a "List of Pieces in this Volume," which gives the plays in the order in which they were bound. On the sides of each volume were stamped his arms in gilt; the spine was lettered "Theatre of Geo. 3." It occurred to me—or possibly to Mr. Massey, I don't recall which—that it would be a pious act of restitution to put the plays back as nearly as possible into the original covers. There had been 58 volumes when the set was sold in 1914, but only 40 of the original covers remained; the rest had been sold off with single plays. Accordingly, it was not possible to put all of the 130 plays back in their original places; some had to go into other covers. This sorting and arranging went on for days, while Mr. Massey, who suffered cruelly from asthma, stood by my side and talked about books and bookselling.

There was a notable interruption the morning Dr. Rosenbach came into the shop. He had been making history by buying up most of the Britwell Court books at Sotheby's with bidding so unconventional and successful that he had not endeared himself to the trade. Instead of sitting at the long tables with the other booksellers and indicating his bids silently, he stood up by the pulpit in which the auctioneer sat and called out his bids in a loud voice. I went to see him bid one day. A lot was put up and advanced by five-shilling stages to three pounds. Rosenbach, who was chatting to a friend, turned to the auctioneer (Mr. Charles Des Graz) and said: "Seven pounds!" The bidding resumed its canonical course until it reached ten pounds, when Rosenbach broke off his conversation long enough to bid "Twenty pounds!" From there on, the trade proceeded by pound jumps, all noiselessly conveyed, to thirty pounds. At that point Rosenbach turned around. He had had enough. "Seventy pounds!" he shouted. "Seventy pounds," repeated Des Graz unperturbed. "Seventy pounds?" He looked around the room. Then he brought down his hammer. "Seventy pounds."

"Excuse me, sir," said Mr. Massey, when the greatest bookseller the world has ever known appeared on that March morning, "but I'm afraid I must attend to him." Mr. Chatto, who sat behind a glass partition at the back of the shop, hurried out to take Mr. Massey's place, but did not look at the visitor. He stood with his back to him. "Please don't bother about me," I said to him. Mr. Chatto shook his head and assumed an air of absorption in the table before us. Although the room was so cold I kept my winter overcoat on, I noticed that he was perspiring freely.

"Have you any Folios?" Rosenbach asked quietly, referring to the Four Folios of Shakespeare. A good First Folio had recently sold for £12,000. Five minutes later Dr. Rosenbach left, having bought a Third Folio for thirty times the amount I was to spend on the collection of plays, the sale of which was to take days. Mr. Chatto returned to his office. Mr. Massey hurried back to me full of apologies. "Very sorry, sir," he said, "but I had to wait on him."

Having at last got the plays into twenty-four of Walpole's original covers, we sent them off to Mr. Bayntun of Bath and had them re-bound. This re-binding seemed the thing to do at the time, but it was a mistake, as became evident four years later when more of the plays turned up in New York, at the Brick Row Bookshop. All the plays I looked at in the Brick Row happened to have a note in Walpole's hand on the title-page or cuttings from newspapers that he dated and pasted upon the plays' flyleaves, but when I looked over the entire collection at Farmington, I found that only about thirty of the plays had been so marked. Many proved to have been printed before 1760, and so could never have been a part of the "Theatre of Geo. 3," but others, as I sadly handled them, began to glow with hidden significance. They, too, had been untimely ripped from volumes, and the *disjecta membra* of their former bindings were hanging from their spines. Fortunately, Mr. Massey had prevailed upon me in 1928 to buy the broken covers of the original set. These now showed conclusively that the plays before me that were printed from 1760 on had come from the "Theatre of Geo. 3." Bits and pieces of their bindings matched the elaborate tooling on the Walpolian spines of those bindings that were virtually intact. This discovery not only supplied thirty more plays, but showed that, contrary to what we had supposed, Walpole did not annotate every play in his collection. Since Dudley and Watson had brought up from the cellar only those plays that bore a note in Walpole's hand, this meant that undoubtedly there were more plays from the "Theatre of Geo. 3" without Walpole's notes in Pickering & Chatto's cellar.

"How," I wrote Dudley Massey, who had succeeded Mr. Chatto and his father as the head of the firm, "are we to identify these plays? Maggs were wicked to break up the set, but haven't you by cleaning off the spines and covering them with your neat little manila wrappers removed the sole remaining means of proving that they were in Walpole's collection?" There was one further proof, he replied, the staining on the edges. Eighteenth-century binders used a red, brown, green, or blue stain on the edges of their books, applying it with a plain, marbled, or sprinkled effect. No two volumes had precisely the same stain, but obviously the staining on all the plays in each volume would be the same. If I went through Walpole's lists of the plays in each volume and sent him the titles of those still missing, he would send me copies of any that they had and I could match them up with my copies of the plays that had been in the volumes with them.

This we did. The lists Walpole made on the front covers I had found named about 420 plays. Some 150 of these were missing. I sent a list of them to Dudley Massey, who mailed to me on approval the copies of them that he had in stock. It was possible to tell at a glance those that were "right," particularly if one compared the lower edges, which had been protected from light and dirt by the shelves on which they stood. Brown and light green applied with a sprinkled effect were the colors used by Walpole's binder on the edges. The staining test identified sixty-five more plays.

A further proof of the plays' identity was provided by the angle test. Since the back of a book is slightly rounded in the binding, its fore-edge becomes concave. This results in the fore-edges at the front and rear of the book acquiring an angle, while those in the middle remain even. As the plays were bound in the order listed by Walpole on the front covers, the fore-edges of those first mentioned should slant inward and those last mentioned should slant outward, while those in the middle should be straight. The angle test, which Chapman called "the Farthest North in bibliography," was a complete success: all the "right" plays slanted exactly as they ought to do. Then, when I was convinced that the play had been in the "Theatre of Geo. 3," I pulled off the manila wrapper and found that the stitching coincided precisely with the stitching in the other plays originally in the volume, and that, final proof, faint remains of the original binding still clung to the plays' narrow spines.

Shortly after the Brick Row cache appeared, I wrote to Pickering & Chatto for a list of the plays that they had sold before I appeared in 1925. Their list (in Watson's fine hand) contains 64 plays, 37 of which I marked with an H. At the top of the list I wrote: "H = Hopeless." These were plays that had been sold to American libraries, the Folger-Shakespeare Library in Washington and the University of Michigan, chiefly. Of these 37 "hopeless" plays, 33, together with many plays not on the Pickering & Chatto list, have come from these libraries and are now at Farmington.

The first of the "Hopeless" plays to reach Farmington were two at Yale. Mr. Andrew Keogh, the then Librarian, handed them over to me, knowing that one day they would return to Yale with the rest of my collection. When I asked him if he thought Michigan might follow suit, he wrote to the Librarian, Mr. W. W. Bishop, on my behalf. The request was unusual, but after consultation with the Michigan authorities Mr. Bishop agreed to let me have them. I returned duplicates and (since Walpole's copies were worth more than ordinary copies) paid the original bill. When after several years I was unable to find duplicates of some of the plays, Mr. Bishop generously allowed me to substitute photostats of the missing plays for the duplicate copies I had contracted to supply. In all, twenty-two plays have come to Farmington from Ann Arbor. Later a similar arrangement was concluded for the two plays at the

University of Illinois. All of these copies had one or more of Walpole's notes in them. Doubtless there are others of his copies without his notes in these libraries.[1]

The Folger Library offered a more difficult problem, which took twelve years to solve. J. Q. Adams, the late Director of the Folger, became convinced that it was in the best interests of all concerned that I should have the plays, but the terms of Folger's will made it difficult to dispose of any books in his library. Several years later I got the corrected proof sheets of Steevens's and Reed's folio edition of Shakespeare. They "belonged" to the Folger as much as its copies of Walpole's plays (all of which it had in other copies) "belonged" to me. This was clear to everyone. So, the trustees concurring, my Shakespeare proof sheets went to the Folger Library and its plays came to me; and then, for good measure, Dr. Adams let me have Walpole's copy of Sheridan's *Critic*, which he had in his own library.

I always called on him when in Washington. He was a scholar who was a humanist; a bookman who read books; a librarian who had secured for his library one of the finest collections of printed books (the Harmsworth library of English books to 1641)

---

[1] Since writing this, seven more have turned up in the Yale Library, three with notes and four without them.

ever brought to this country. My call in April 1939, after the exchange of the proof sheets and plays was completed, was a particularly pleasant one. Then, when I rejoined my wife in the exhibition gallery of the library, she pointed silently to a case, and there was another play, not included in the just-completed transaction, Walpole's copy of *Timon of Athens*, 1771, restored to the original Strawberry Hill covers —which meant that it contained another "List of Pieces in this Volume" in Walpole's hand. I hurried back to Adams. "Heaven knows how many more of Walpole's plays we have!" he said. "We shan't finish our catalogue for years. Have you ever been down in the stacks?" I hadn't, and he asked Giles Dawson to show them to me.

The stacks in the basement have thousands of plays, all bound in manila wrappers. We walked slowly along the central aisle. At one point I paused, turned into a side aisle, looked along a shelf of identically bound plays, took one down, opened it, and there on the title-page was a note in Walpole's hand.

When the Folger Library was finally catalogued, some two dozen volumes from Strawberry Hill, as well as additional plays from the "Theatre of Geo. 3," had appeared, including Walpole's copy of the Second Folio. I had run out of Shakespearean proof sheets and had nothing else worthy of the Folger.

Why shouldn't it sell me its books from Walpole's library if they were duplicates and be done with it? The question was put to the chairman of the library's board, Chief Justice Stone, who approved the transfer just a week before he died. With the money it received for the duplicates, the library was able to buy a picture that it could not otherwise have had, a reproduction of the Chandos portrait of Shakespeare made for Edmond Malone before it was retouched. "In my judgment," wrote Adams, "this is far more valuable to students than the Chandos portrait as it now is. And the price we paid was almost exactly the same represented by your check. Thanks!"

2

Three hundred and fifty of the plays (about two thirds of the collection) have been reassembled at Farmington, with about four fifths of the original bindings and the unbroken volume of Prologues and Epilogues, which Walpole collected from 1780 on and pasted into a separate volume. (This was the volume that was given to me by Mrs. E. P. Merritt after her husband's death in 1933.) The whereabouts of fifteen more plays are known; four of them are bound in the original sides from which they were removed and are at Harvard in the Merritt Collection; one volume is also there intact, the Plays of William

List of pieces in this Volume.

Account of ruins in the highlands.
Prospect from Barrow-hill.
Transaction between D. North & D. of Gordon.
Two letters from Mr Burke.
On the abuse of unrestrained power.
Substance of General Burgoyne's speeches.
Anticipation. by Mr Tickell.
Mr Bryant's Answer, on his Analysis.
Three letters from Sr J. Dalrymple to D. Barington.
Mr Gibbon's Vindication of the 15th & 16th Chapters.
Considerations on the state of affairs.
Barretti's Introduction to the Carmen Seculare.
Mr Walpole's letter on Chatterton.

Davies, together with the title-pages that Walpole had printed for the first eleven volumes.

The "Theatre of Geo. 3" throws light on Walpole's plan to write the history of his time. By 1760, when George III came to the throne, Walpole had been secretly working on his project ten years. With the accession of a young prince who gave promise of being a patron of the arts and letters, Walpole took his *Memoirs* even more seriously. To do the job thoroughly, he began collecting contemporary plays, poems, and tracts as they appeared. His intention was to show the thought and life of his time, not just to give an abstract of foreign and Parliamentary news. These "Geo. 3" collections were of some use to him in writing his *Memoirs;* they were of great use to him in writing his letters; they have been of even greater use to his editors, for most of them have come safely to port: the poems in quarto, 22 volumes, are at Harvard; the only known volume of "Poems of Geo. 3" in octavo is at Farmington; the "Tracts of Geo. 3," 59 volumes in quarto and octavo, are also there. Many of Walpole's letters refer to pieces in these collections.

I first heard about the "Tracts of Geo. 3" from William A. Jackson in 1935. They were then in the library of Sir Leicester Harmsworth at Bexhill in Kent. On his death in 1939, his trustees sold it to me, together with 88 volumes of earlier tracts formerly at

Strawberry Hill, through Quaritch. This collection is more important than the "Theatre of Geo. 3," and more useful; it is larger; it is unbroken; I had to wait only three years before getting it; but as an exercise in collecting, it was mild compared with the mutilated "Theatre of Geo. 3."

Walpole's "Geo. 3" collections indirectly inspired a twentieth-century project. The willingness of so many American libraries to exchange Walpole's copies of plays suggested an ambitious experiment in library co-operation.

Early in 1942 a group of librarians and collectors was formed to assist the Librarian of Congress during the war. There were twenty-four of us from all parts of the country. Among the subjects that we discussed was the ever pressing problem of housing the spate of books that deluges the modern world. No library is rich enough or has room enough for anything like the books it wishes to own. At an executive-committee meeting at Farmington in October 1942 (I was chairman of the group), Keyes D. Metcalf, the Director of the Harvard Libraries, undertook to study how libraries might co-operate with each other to ensure that there would be at least two copies of all foreign printed books somewhere in the United States. We suggested that the great research libraries might join to buy all the books in certain fields—Yale in chemistry, for example, Cornell in Icelandic literature, and so on. In this way the libraries would be freed from the impossible task of trying to get all the books on every subject under the sun. Because of the efficient system of inter-library loans in this country, scholars who want to use out-of-the-way books can do so with little delay. Thanks to Mr. Metcalf, this plan, which is called the Farmington Plan because of its place of origin, has become a part of American library policy. The immediate benefits of it are obvious; less apparent is the salutary spirit it fosters of co-operation as opposed to rivalry. Emulation and parochialism, the "Boola Boola" spirit, had their uses when we were an immature country living to ourselves. Now that we hold so many of the earth's greatest treasures and have discovered that the world is round, it is pleasant to learn that we dare to be generous. At present the Farmington Plan is applied only to contemporary books printed in "the Farmington countries" of Europe—France, Belgium, Holland, Switzerland, Sweden, and others. It is too much to expect that libraries will transfer their *rariora* in any wholesale manner, yet they have done so at least once in a retail manner, as the unfinished saga of the "Theatre of Geo. 3" relates.

X

I

IT IS an easy step from collecting the books that belonged to "your" man to collecting other objects owned by him. Such an object is called a "relic." The *Oxford Dictionary's* shade of meaning that comes nearest to the collector's use of the word is: "An object invested with interest by reason of its antiquity or associations with the past," and, above all, it should be added, with a person. Shelley's guitar in the Bodleian is a relic; Dr. Johnson's teapot, which was formerly A. E. Newton's and now belongs to Donald Hyde, is a relic. They communicate the sense of intimacy that the collector seeks.

Strawberry Hill was filled with relics: Cardinal Wolsey's hat, the spurs worn by King William at the Battle of the Boyne, James I's gloves. It also had examples of that class of relic which is much in favor with collectors, hair. When Walpole visited Saint-Cyr, the convent founded by Mme de Maintenon for the education of noblemen's daughters, a nun presented him with "a piece of Mme de Maintenon's own writing" and a lock of her hair. They are before me now. *"Il faut s'enthousiasmer,"* Walpole wrote Mme du Deffand of this visit, *"à de certaines visions, comme je fais, sans quoi tout est fade."* Walpole had other hair, all of it irreproachable. He kept his mother's and father's in two lockets in the shape of hearts set with diamonds; he had a bit of the hair of Mary Tudor, Queen of France, which he acquired when her tomb was opened at St. Edmundsbury in 1784; five years later when Edward V's coffin was discovered, Sir Joseph Banks, the president of the Royal Society, gave Walpole a few wisps of the King's hair. Hair is a powerful evoker of visions. Certain dealers go in for it, enshrining it, as did Walpole, in jeweled lockets. Shelley (who had a fine head of hair) is a favorite with hair-collectors and so is Napoleon (who had less hair, but kept it longer). Of all relics hair is perhaps the truest: because its genuineness is the most dubious, the purchaser demands reasonable assurance of its authenticity.

I have, I am sorry to say, no wisp of Horace Walpole's hair, nor do I know of anyone who has. His bones lie sealed in the crypt of the chapel at Houghton, that much we do know, and there may have been until 1941 an object of clinical wonder in the Royal College of Surgeons in Lincoln's Inn Fields. Walpole wrote on October 5, 1793: "I have been ill of the gout in four or five parts, and produced from one of my fingers a chalkstone, that I believe is worthy of a place in Mr. Hunter's collection of human miseries—he best knows whether it is qualified to be a candidate there—I do know that on delivery, I had it weighed and its weight was four grains and a half; and with two detached bits, five grains." Did Walpole by any chance give this chalkstone to John Hunter for his museum? We shall never know, for the catalogue of the museum is incomplete and its specimens perished when the museum was bombed in 1941.

Although there seems to be no remnant of Horace Walpole's person, we know of thousands of objects that were associated with him. "You would laugh," he wrote in 1756, "if you saw in the midst of what trumpery I am writing. Two reporters have just brought home my purchases from Mrs. Kennon the midwife's sale: Brobdignag combs, old broken pots, pans, and pipkins, a lantern of scraped oyster-shells, scimitars, Turkish pipes, Chinese baskets, etc., etc. . . . P.S. I forgot that I was outbid for Oliver Cromwell's nightcap." All these—and the other contents of Strawberry Hill—have in their turn become relics.

As the drawings of Strawberry Hill "raise pleasing sensations," so also does its "dry list of curiosities." The *Description* makes it clear what the eighteenth-century parties of four—the limit for a day—saw

MME DU DEFFAND'S
SNUFFBOX

CABINET DESIGNED FOR
LADY DIANA BEAUCLERK'S
DRAWINGS

when they were being shown through the house by the housekeeper or the master himself, while the dogs barked and raced about. The account of the china, porcelains, and glass in one of the smallest rooms in the house, the China Closet (twelve by nine feet), alone fills thirteen pages, quarto, in the 1784 *Description*, and about each and every article there was something to say. Macaulay, who was often at Strawberry before its contents were dispersed, wrote that "There is a story about the fire tongs and another about the bell-rope." Everyone seems to have been exhausted when the tour of the house was over, except the housekeeper, Margaret Young, who pocketed the four guineas handed her by the four departing visitors as a just tribute to her memory and tirelessness.

The identification of many of the contents of the house, which are now scattered about the world, is certain because of Walpole's habit of writing on the backs of his pictures, prints, and drawings and of having inscriptions placed upon objects of art. On the inside of the door of a Strawberry Hill cabinet at Farmington is a gold plaque that states: "This Cabinet was ordered by and made at the Expense of Mr. Horace Walpole in 1784, to receive the Drawings which were all designed and executed by the Right Honourable Lady Diana Beauclerc. The Cabinet was design'd by Mr. E. Edwards." He wished to give future historians all possible aid in studying the eighteenth century. Inside the lid of one of his snuffboxes Walpole had inscribed: "This snuff box, with the portrait of her dog Tonton, was bequeathed by Mme la Marquise du Deffand to Mr. Horace Walpole, 1780."

Most of the objects at Strawberry Hill can be identified by means of two books. The first is Walpole's *Description of Strawberry Hill*; the second is *A Catalogue of the Classic Contents of Strawberry Hill Collected by Horace Walpole*. Of the many anniversaries that went uncelebrated because of the war, that which fell on April 25, 1942 was, for Walpolians, the most memorable. One hundred years earlier began the sale that shredded out and undid the labor of a lifetime— and, incidentally, gave posterity the delightful job of trying to do it all over again. "The valuable contents of Strawberry Hill, it may fearlessly be proclaimed," said the Sale Catalogue, formed "the most distinguished gem that has ever adorned the annals of auctions," and "a repast for the Lovers of Literature and the Fine Arts, of which bygone days furnish no previous example, and it would be in vain to contemplate it in times to come." Although this lushness invited derisive comment, the newspapers gave lengthy accounts of the thousands of persons who visited Strawberry on the days before the sale and were particular in naming all those above the rank of viscount. The roads leading to Twickenham were choked with carriages; a boat brought many more who had no carriages.

I have over thirty copies of these Sale Catalogues. Many of them have notes made by their owners at the sale. The margins of the catalogues are often covered with information not found elsewhere; many catalogues are interleaved with prints and drawings and cuttings from newspapers, magazines, and later sale catalogues. Nineteenth-century Walpolians were more numerous than has been realized.

Thanks to my sixty-odd copies of the *Description* and the Sale Catalogue, and the index at Farmington made from them of every object at Strawberry Hill, I can enjoy "the transient pleasure" that Walpole surmised might "hereafter arise to the peruser of this catalogue," if a pleasure can be called "transient" that has grown steadily stronger during twenty-five years. "The Farnese Hercules in wax, by Gosset"; "Two kittens in marble, by Mrs. Damer"; "An Egyptian pebble, with a *lusus naturae* that represents Voltaire in his nightgown and cap"; these and thousands of other objects crowded the thirty rooms and passageways of the house. I confess that I can read this sort of thing endlessly—not only read it, but try to follow the subsequent history of each and every piece as if it were the Grail itself. For a year an Englishwoman searched Christie's, the auctioneer's, records for me to note all reappearances in their sale rooms of objects formerly at Strawberry. It almost seemed as if a special providence were looking after the success of the undertaking, for after she completed her long task and handed the ledgers back to the owners, after she had thanked them for their courtesy and co-operation, picked up her bag and gloves and the hundreds of notes she had made, after she left the building that night, Christie's and its contents were destroyed in an air-raid.

The *Description* and the Sale Catalogue prove Walpole's ownership of many pieces that he did not inscribe himself. When Sir Osbert Sitwell told me that he had two plates of faïence with the stories of Cain and Abel and Abraham and Isaac and that he wanted to give them to me if they really had been Walpole's, the Sale Catalogue reassured us completely. Should the "tortoise-shell case, mounted with silver, in which the celebrated Admiral Van Tromp used to carry his pipes to sea" turn up, we could recognize it, and probably also a "needle case in fine old Japan with Monkeys." The Sale Catalogue would help us with hundreds of objects, but it is hardly enough for scores of others. "A broken patera" is inadequate, and so is "an antique cow." Still, one can never tell what the next copy of the *Description* or Sale Catalogue may reveal.

154

One might suppose that there was little more to be discovered, but my most recent copy of the *Description* cleared up a mystery. In the 1774 *Description* Walpole mentioned "Fourteen small Etruscan vases and Ten black Staffordshire ditto" that were in the Little Library in the Cottage in the Garden. In the 1784 *Description* in the same place we read merely of "Several small Etruscan and black Staffordshire vases." What has happened? Is everything all right? The answer is found in my thirty-fifth copy of the *Description*, Walpole's "key" copy, in which he wrote thousands of words to correct and annotate the text. Opposite the entries about the Etruscan and Staffordshire vases he made it plain that everything was not all right: "Some of the vases over the books were broken in 1777," he wrote, "by an owl that fell down the chimney."

2

The first relics I ever bought were the chairs that belonged to Dr. Johnson, the pillow made for William Blake by his wife, Gainsborough's easel, and Charles Lamb's tea caddy, all of them "wrong." The humiliation of that experience temporarily cooled my enthusiasm for relics. It revived one day in February 1925 when, killing half an hour in the library of the University Club in New York, I looked for the first time in my life at an auction-sale catalogue of

pictures. It was the catalogue of the Arthur Tooth
Sale, which was held that night. Lot 26 was a portrait
of a Lady Mary Churchill, by, the catalogue said,
Francis Cotes. I realized that there was doubtless more
than one Lady Mary Churchill in the eighteenth century, but Walpole had a half-sister of that name, and
I, who had been collecting Walpole for three months,
hurried to the Anderson Galleries to see lot 26.

The portrait is a half-length of a woman of about
thirty, leaning on an open music book. She has a veil
over her head and is wearing a green velvet dress
upon which is a brooch with an enormous diamond.
"Lady Mary Churchill" is painted on the canvas.
Lady Mary was the natural daughter of Sir Robert
Walpole by the woman who subsequently became his
second wife. If the gossip about Horace Walpole's
being the son of a Hervey were true, Horace Walpole
and Lady Mary Churchill would be no blood relation and would, presumably, have no physical resemblance. This portrait of Lady Mary shows that she
might have been Horace Walpole's twin. I bought it
with only one opposing bid. When I got it home, I
went through the *Strawberry Hill Catalogue* looking
for a description of my picture. I found it among the
family portraits in the Great Parlour, Twenty-first
Day's Sale, lot 39: "A half length of Lady Maria Walpole, only child of Sir Robert and Maria Skerret,

and wife of Charles Churchill, only son of General
Churchill. Eckardt. She is represented in a veil, with
a music book before her, a very charming picture."

Eckardt was a young German who had been
brought to England by Jean Baptiste Vanloo. Eckardt was very useful to Walpole, who as a young
man could not afford more expensive artists and who
wanted portraits of some two dozen of his friends
for Strawberry Hill. Walpole also addressed a poem,
"The Beauties," to Eckardt (or Eccardt, as perhaps
he should be spelled), and did what he could to
launch him as a fashionable portrait-painter, but
without much success. (At their best his pictures pass
for early pictures by Francis Cotes.) Eccardt's portrait of Lady Mary remains the chief link with that
tantalizingly dim woman. We can be certain that
Walpole planned it, as he planned Eccardt's portraits
of Gray, Bentley, himself, and the rest. The details
of Lady Mary's portrait are therefore significant—the
music book, for example. "Lady Mary," Walpole
wrote to Mann, "has a remarkable knowledge of music and can sing," which she did to her own accom-
paniment on the harpsichord. A second striking de-
tail, the enormous diamond brooch, is explained in
another letter to Mann, which was written forty-one
years after the first. Lord Hardwicke had just repeated the old charge that George II gave Sir Robert

Walpole a large sum of money toward building Houghton, the huge Walpole house in Norfolk. "For presents," writes Walpole, "the king never made Sir Robert any but two, one of which was a very large diamond, but with a great flaw in it, which Lady Mary had." There is no doubt, I think, that this is the diamond Lady Mary is wearing in the brooch that Eccardt painted with such fidelity.

3

Relics and association items furnish the collector with his most dramatic stories. Resisting the temptation to astonish, I'll add only two.

Shortly before we left for home in 1935, Mr. R. M. Holland Martin asked us down to Worcestershire for a week-end. It seemed that a great house in his neighborhood had many relics formerly at Strawberry Hill. Frequent disappointment has cautioned me against transports on hearing such news, but there is always the possibility that it is true, and the collector must not ignore it.

The first thing that we saw when we walked into the hall of the Tudor castle was the familiar set of Holbein's drawings of Jane Seymour, Colet, and the rest. Were they the copies made by Vertue for the Holbein Chamber at Strawberry? I asked. The owner not being sure, we clambered on chairs, got the

Lanthorn at Strawberryhill.

THE LANTERN, FROM BENTLEY'S DRAWING

drawings down, and found that Walpole had written long notes on the back of all of them.

The house was filled with Walpolian relics. The fine Mabeuse of Henry VII's marriage was there, miniatures of Henry VIII's Queens by Holbein, "Hangings for a State Bed." Our host showed me a list of the Strawberry relics. As I copied it off I came to "Gothic lanthorn." "Is that the famous Gothic lantern?" I asked.

"I don't know whether it's the famous Gothic lantern or not, but it is the ugliest blasted lantern that ever was."

That sounded like it, and I said, truthfully, that I would rather see it than anything in England, that I had Bentley's original design for it and drawings of it after Walpole had fitted it with bits of painted glass, some of it English glass of the early fifteenth century. It hung in the stair-well at Strawberry Hill and was admired by visitors from all over Europe.

"I am afraid," replied its owner, "that you have come too late."

I was appalled, and said so.

"My wife wouldn't have it hanging about any longer and threw it out."

"Threw it out!"

"It just may not have gone."

We hurried away through the house and through

the cloisters to a lumber room. There on a bench next to the door and oblivion stood the lantern, the epitome of Strawberry Hill and the neo-Gothic movement, a flimsy thing with a tin cross, ugly and original, a story connected with each of its bits of painted glass.

"Well," said the wife of the owner, who had joined us, "I won't have it back in the house. Perhaps we should give it to the Cheltenham Museum."

"What should I do now?" I asked Mr. Holland Martin as we rode away. On his advice I wrote to the owner to say that if he and his wife ever decided to get rid of the lantern, I hoped that they would let me know about it. The lantern is now at Farmington, where, alas, it is also in disfavor with its chatelaine; but relics should be reserved for the faithful, and it is fitting that the lantern should cast its electric beam only upon those who are willing to seek it out, well removed from the ordinary life of the house, in the book stacks.

Walpole's Berkeley Square house was torn down in 1937 to make way for the Air Ministry. We know comparatively little about the house, but Walpole had lived and died there, and rather than have it sink without a trace, I decided to have something from it. The owners of it in the twenties once told me that

WALPOLE'S BERKELEY SQUARE HOUSE ABOUT 1910

at the time of the Gordon Riots in 1780, when the
mob broke into Lord Mansfield's house and burned
his great library, Walpole reinforced the door of his
own house with iron bars. He says nothing about the
bars in his letters, which show that, far from being
terrified by the riots, he rather enjoyed them, but *"il
faut s'enthousiasmer."* The door was more manage-
able than a flight of stairs or a chimney would have
been; the door I decided to have. Sproule of Pickering & Chatto kindly offered to get it from the wreck-
ers for me and did so, not revealing for whom he was
acting. This is the sort of story that flourishes in the
English "silly season." It was printed in the London
papers and reprinted all over England, as we learned
from friends who sent us cuttings from their local
papers. The story even pursued us to the middle of
the Atlantic, where one morning we read in the
"boiler plate" part of the *Mid-Ocean News* that the
door to Walpole's house in Berkeley Square had been
bought, in the familiar English phrase, by "an eccentric American millionaire" and taken to America.

The relic lay forgotten in its crate for eleven years,
until 1948, when we added the two stack rooms to the
library and my wife remembered the door in our
cellar. We decided to use it, not as a door, but in
place of a wall that would otherwise have had to be
built. This was done, but not until after an awk-

wardness had been corrected. The back of the door does have iron bars, and, throwing historical nicety to the winds, I told the contractor who was building the new rooms the story of the bars as it had been told to me. These eighteenth-century bars and the occasion that allegedly inspired their use worked so powerfully on his imagination that when the door was put in place the bars were outward and the handsome paneled door inward and invisible. When you deal with relics of such power as this door, anything can happen.

XI

I

PRODUCING BOOKS follows naturally from collecting them, particularly if one has a frustrated literary or scholarly bent. As the collector gets deeper into his subject, he becomes aware that in his own collection is a book or manuscript, print or map, whose significance has not been revealed. He sees himself bringing this tasty morsel to the feast of learning and receiving glances of approval from the diners. In publishing it he may be stirred by something nobler than pride of possession; he may feel that he is putting his collection to work and justifying the time and thought and money he has spent upon it.

In 1772 Walpole printed at Strawberry Hill two numbers of what he called *Miscellaneous Antiquities; or, A Collection of Curious Papers: Either republished from Scarce Tracts, or now first printed from Original MSS. To be Continued Occasionally.* His "Advertisement by the Editors" explained that "The taste for anecdotes and historic papers . . . was never more general than at present." He printed 500 copies of the first two numbers for sale, with 25 more on writing-paper for presents. Only 130 copies were sold. "I cannot afford to make the town perpetual presents," Walpole wrote, and gave up *Miscellaneous Antiquities.*

One hundred and fifty-five years later I had the temerity to revive it. The plan appealed to Edwin B. Rudge, who brought out *Miscellaneous Antiquities, Number Three, A Notebook of Horace Walpole,* in a printing of 500 copies. This little manuscript (a thirty-twomo) was worth printing. Walpole kept it from 1780 to 1783, writing in it random thoughts and notes on contemporary events, many of which he worked into his letters. In the notebook, for example, he recorded: "Launcelot Brown, Gardenist, died Feb. 6, 1783, at his son-in-law Holland's door in Hertford Street." On February 8 Walpole wrote Lady Ossory: "Your dryads must go into black gloves, Madam: their father-in-law, Lady Nature's second husband, is dead! Mr. Brown dropped down at his own door yesterday." Two days later he wrote to Mason: "I have a mind, should you approve it, to call designers of gardens, *gardenists,* to distinguish them from *gardeners* or *landscapists.*" Rudge reproduced the notebook in facsimile and issued it in a cloth box that imitated the leather box in which a nineteenth-century owner had put it. I transcribed the text and

164

showed how Walpole used it in his letters. It was of my transcription and its errors that Chapman wrote: "It really won't do."

The following year the American Branch of the Oxford University Press brought out *Miscellaneous Antiquities, Number Four, Lady Louisa Stuart's Notes on Jesse's George Selwyn and His Contemporaries*, also in a printing of 500 copies. Daniel Berkeley Updike, of the Merrymount Press, designed and printed it, and it was chosen as one of the "Fifty Books" of 1928. This time the text was correct. For Number Five I edited a large collection of unpublished letters to George Selwyn that I had acquired, but abandoned this project for an edition of Horace Walpole's *Fugitive Verses*. This was also published by Oxford in an edition of 500 copies. Each of my three numbers sold almost exactly the same number of copies as had Walpole's, about 130. Like him, I gave up trying to satisfy the public taste in antiquities, but I continued the series until 1941 by privately printing (at the Hawthorn Press) unpublished odds and ends from my collection, in editions of 50 and 100 copies, which I gave away as Christmas presents.

In the middle of 1932 I set myself to a formidable task, that of making an index to Walpole's journal of his five visits to Paris in 1765–75. The journal was one of the manuscripts that Mr. and Mrs. Merritt generously put at my disposal. It is largely made up of lists of persons Walpole met during his Paris visits. There may be thirty or forty names in an entry. For example, on December 17, 1765, after mentioning eighteen people, Walpole "supped at Mme de Luxembourg's with the Prince of Conti, Mme de Boufflers, Mme de Mirepoix, Mme de Maurevel, Mme du Deffand, Duchesse and Mlle de Boufflers, Mr. Hume, Mr. Craufurd, Marquis de Montmorency, and Baron de Wimpffen. Mme du Deffand said of Lady Sandwich, she employed the strength of Samson to tear a piece of paper." Identifying the members of such a supper party took me hours in the beginning. The Boufflers ladies were a considerable problem in themselves. There were seven of them: (1) Marie-Charlotte-Hippolyte de Camps de Saujon, who married Édouard, Comte (Marquis 1751) de Boufflers-Rouverel; (2) her daughter-in-law, Amélie-Constance Puchot des Allers, who married Louis-Édouard Comte de Boufflers; (3) Marie-Anne-Philippine Thérèse de Montmorency Duchesse de Boufflers; (4) Madeleine-Angélique de Neufville Duchesse de Boufflers; (5) Marie-Françoise-Catherine de Beauveau-Craon Marquise de Boufflers; (6) Amélie de Boufflers; (7) Françoise-Éléonore de Jean de Manville, Mme de Stanislas-Jean de Boufflers. Getting these people straight so that when Walpole referred to Mme or Mlle de Boufflers I could be certain which woman he meant took time.

Other families were even more difficult: twenty-eight Montmorencys, thirty-three Bourbons, thirty-five Choiseuls had to be disinterred in the French peerages, which are much less helpful than the English. In the beginning, only my belief that this was a life-and-death test of my character and endurance kept me at it. Then, gradually, these names took on meaning as their owners came to life, and I was able to discriminate the figures in what Mme du Deffand called *"une société infernale."* I was six months completing Walpole's first visit (which lasted six months and occupies about half his Parisian Journal). It was later done much better by Warren Smith, but my struggle with the *ancien régime* proved to be the most salutary exercise I have ever undergone.

It was followed by one that also took six months. William M. Ivins, Jr., asked me to write a monograph for the *Metropolitan Museum Studies* on Strawberry Hill. I chose the subject "The Genesis of Strawberry Hill," which, because of Walpole's letters, Bentley's drawings, and Walpole's extra-illustrated copy of his *Description,* could be traced with confidence and fully illustrated. In my paper I referred to four missing drawings, not executed, that Robert Adam made for a cottage in the garden. "They will doubtless turn up in time," I wrote, "and then I believe we shall see another unfulfilled Strawberry dream." They turned up the following year in the shop of my friend X, and the dream they reveal is an uneasy one.

2

The reader may recall that in 1929 I suggested rather jocosely to Chapman and Milford that they should publish a new edition of Walpole's letters. At that time I had in mind the need for printing the letters to Walpole and for annotating both sides of his correspondence so that a modern reader would know what he and his friends were talking about.

Only a few hundred letters to Walpole had ever been printed with his letters, although some fifteen hundred had been printed independently. To print only one side of a correspondence is like listening to one side of a telephone conversation where the invisible partner to it is a stranger. Walpole's letters cannot be thoroughly studied or appreciated without the letters to which they are an answer, whether his correspondents were informative, entertaining, or dull. The letters to Walpole put his letters back into their original context.

The second reason why we needed a new edition

was even more obvious: the letters should be annotated with the fullness that the most informative record of the eighteenth century deserves. Walpole's letters had been printed over and over again since 1798,
but, except for Paget Toynbee's three Supplements,
with hardly any elucidation at all. Mrs. Toynbee
identified the people who are in *The Dictionary of
National Biography* and *Complete Peerage*, but did
little more, yet the case for full annotation had been
made in 1848 by John Wilson Croker when review-
ing Vernon Smith's edition of Walpole's letters to
Lady Ossory: "What the reader most indispensably
needs, and what registers and magazines cannot supply, is the explanation of small events, slight allusions, obscure anecdotes, traits of individual characters, the gossip of the circle, and all the little items
and accidents of domestic, social, and political life,
which constitute in a most peculiar degree the staple
of Walpole's correspondence—the most frequent occasions and chief objects of either his wit or his sagacity, and without some knowledge of which his best
letters would be little more than a collection of
riddles."

As time went on, my wife and I took the possibility of editing a new edition of Walpole's correspondence more and more seriously; so much so that our
trip to England in September 1932 was in the nature

of a decisive step. One day that year, while talking to
Mr. Ernest Maggs in his shop, it occurred to me that
I should have an example of Walpole's hand every
year of his life. I bought the fifty-odd Walpole letters
and manuscripts the firm had in stock, the other
Walpole letters that were in the London shops, and,
on our return home, the Walpole letters that were in
New York shops, a total of about one hundred letters.
At that time the reputation of the Toynbee edition
was so high that it seemed impertinent to collate its
text with the original letters, but I did so and was as-
tonished to find that there were errors in almost every
letter, errors in proper names and dates. Frequently
formal conclusions had been chopped off by the first
editors; addresses and postmarks had been omitted
from all the letters except those edited by Toynbee
in his last Supplement; many passages had been left
out through careless transcription; many had been
expurgated. Lockhart (Scott's biographer) had seen
"some sheets with curious notes of [Miss Berry, Walpole's first editor] in pencil, suggesting adroit methods of softening without obliterating sundry very
gross jokes." Other editors had gone further than a
softening pencil, resorting to scissors and the fire.
The result of this expurgation has been to raise ex-
pectations that the uncensored documents do not ful-
fill. Comparison of the Toynbee text with the origi-

nals made clear a third reason for a new edition: the need of a full and correct text.

The Yale English Department agreed that the new edition would be desirable. To put the project in writing and announce it to the world, Professor Frederick A. Pottle arranged for me to read a fifteen-minute paper at a session of the Modern Language Association in December 1932 on "Proposals for a New Edition of Horace Walpole's Correspondence." While writing it I made the statement that anyone, even if he had spent years reading Horace Walpole's letters, could open the best edition of them at random and, because of its lack of notes, be thoroughly stuck half a dozen times in the first page he read. After writing this I wondered if it were true. I reached out, took down at random Volume VIII of the Toynbee edition, and opened it at pages 264–5 to Walpole's letter of April 7, 1773 to William Cole. It is not the sort of letter that one thinks of as being typically Walpolian: it is not witty or urbane or sagacious or gossipy; there is no passage in it that indicates those tacit assumptions of the day that reveal the manners and mind of the eighteenth century; no character or episode of particular interest to posterity is illuminated. Still, it could not have served my purpose better, for it confirmed my three main points: the text was faulty; Cole's letter to which Walpole was replying is essential to its understanding; the allusions and references in it cannot be understood unless one consults a dozen books, some of which are extremely rare. Furthermore, it showed how "collectors' books" can clear up mysteries that can be solved in no other way.

Here is the letter as it appears in Toynbee:

I have now seen the second volume of the Archæologia, *or Old Women's Logic, with Mr. Master's answer to me. If he had not taken such pains to declare it was written against my* Doubts, *I should have thought it a defence of them, for the few facts he quotes make for my arguments, and confute himself; particularly in the case of Lady Eleanor Butler; whom, by the way, he makes marry her own nephew, and not descend from her own family, because she was descended from her grandfather. This Mr. Masters is an excellent Sancho Panza to such a Don Quixote as Dean Milles! but enough of such goosecaps!*

Pray thank Mr. Ashby for his admirable correction of Sir Thomas Wyat's bon mot; it is right beyond all doubt, and I will quote it if ever the piece is reprinted.

Mr. Tyson surprises me by usurping your Dissertation. It seems all is fish that comes into the net of the Society. Mercy on us! What a cart-load of brick and rubbish and Roman ruins they have piled together! I have found nothing tolerable in the volume but the dissertation of Mr. Masters, which is followed by an answer, that, like Masters's, contradicts him, without disproving anything.

Mr. West's books are selling outrageously. His family will make a fortune by what he collected from stalls and Moorfields. But I must not blame the virtuosi, *having surpassed them. In short, I have bought his two pictures of Henry V and Henry VIII and their families, the first of which is engraved in my* Anecdotes, or, as the Catalogue says, engraved by Mr. H. Walpole, *and the second described there. The first cost me £38 and the last £84, though I knew Mr. West bought it for six guineas. But, in fact, these two, with my Marriages of Henry VI and VII, compose such a suite of the house of Lancaster, and enrich my Gothic house so completely, that I would not deny myself. The Henry VII cost me as much, and is less curious; the price of antiquities is so exceedingly risen, too, at present, that I expected to have paid more. I have bought much cheaper at the same sale, a picture of Henry VIII and Charles V in one piece, both much younger than ever I saw any portrait of either. I hope your pilgrimage to* St. Gulaston's *this month will take place, and that you will come and see them. Adieu! dear Sir. Yours ever,*

H. W.

The original of this letter is in the British Museum, together with Cole's copy of his letter to which Walpole was replying. I had photostats of both letters. Collation of the text with the photostat of Walpole's letter showed that there were a dozen trifling errors of transcription and three that would gladden the heart of any scholar examining the work of a predecessor. One of these was a howler: in the third paragraph the first "Masters" should read "Maseres," who was quite a different man. Since all the references to Masters are disparaging and the reference to Maseres is laudatory, the text as it stands is confusing to a degree. The editors probably did not collate their copies with the original letter in the British Museum and they could not have read what they were printing with attention, because it was gibberish. Cole's letter complements Walpole's, as one side of a conversation complements the other; without it three of the allusions in Walpole's letter cannot be understood. Furthermore, Cole's copy of Walpole's letter gives the first sentence in the third paragraph, a passage that has been obliterated in Walpole's original; it also adds a long note on Cole's visit to Strawberry Hill soon after this exchange of letters took place and several relevant particulars. Two points in the letter were made clearer by my having Walpole's

174

annotated sale catalogue of West's pictures. In this catalogue Walpole marked the prices he paid for the pictures and made other notes that contradict what he wrote to Cole. "Collectors' items" may contribute useful footnotes.

I read my paper to the English Group VIII of the Modern Language Association, whose field is the second half of the eighteenth century. "We have a *very* heavy schedule," the chairman kept repeating as he urged us to rattle on faster. When I reached the end of my paper there was a pause for discussion. The only question was: "Will you tell me later some of the expurgated passages?" A discreet titter went around the room.

3

My wife and I were prepared to finance the new edition, but only if it had the backing of a university. Without that endorsement it would be merely the eccentric venture of an amateur who fancied himself a scholar. I wanted the sponsoring university to be Yale, because it was my own university and because of the Yale Library's strength in the literature, county histories, and newspapers of the eighteenth century. For a private collector, I had a large number of reference books, periodicals, and "background" books, but the new edition would require a vast library that dealt exhaustively with every phase of the eighteenth century and earlier times as well.

There was a considerable obstacle to be overcome by the Yale authorities. This was my lack of a Ph.D. It is customary for holders of that degree to speak of it with affectionate contempt, yet they accept it (or a foreign equivalent) as the one and only test for admission to the academic guild. My case was a special one and the cause of some embarrassment, since I was an old friend of most of those who had the decision to make. Could the university recognize a not very young man who was outside the guild, who trotted off to Europe frequently to buy books, and who was thus not only an amateur, but a book-collector as well? Tinker, of course, regarded this last as in my favor, but to others it smacked of dilettantism. It was true that the young man had printed, chiefly at his own expense, several little books on Walpole, but they were pretty slight, and he had published a novel and flirted with the theater. It was not an easy case to decide.

After months of delay Yale appointed me a Research Associate in June 1933. As I look back upon it now, everyone involved in the launching of the *Yale Edition of Horace Walpole's Correspondence* showed courage. Tinker, Pottle, and Karl Young of the Yale English Department, Andrew Keogh, the Librarian, Charles Seymour, and E. S. Furniss, Provost and Dean of the Graduate School, were brave in their endorsement of an outsider. A. Dayle Wallace, who had just emerged from the Graduate School, took a chance of wasting precious years by throwing in his lot as my earliest assistant; and I took a chance of being the leading figure in an expensive fiasco that would stand between me and anything I attempted thereafter. I felt I could carry out the project, however, and no doubt that confidence was helpful to all concerned.

Fourteen volumes of the *Yale Walpole* have appeared since then; work is well along on sixteen more. The final volume (Volume 50?) I hope will be published on November 14, 1965, my seventieth birthday. When the last volume is published, it will be necessary to start right in on the supplementary volumes. These will include letters that will have turned up in correspondences we have passed (there are only two of these letters so far, both to Walpole, but there will be others), and additions and corrections. It is so easy to improve upon a "definitive" work of scholarship that I hope posterity will supplement and correct the *Yale Walpole* to the end of time. Students in the twenty-fifth century (if the race survives until then) will turn to our index (which will fill at least four volumes) for direction to subjects that range from abbots to the battle of Zullichau. I once made the remark that you will find every subject under the sun in Horace Walpole except bee-keeping, and the next unpublished letter I found was all about the keeping of bees, how wasteful the British farmer was who destroyed his bees in securing the honey, how wise—and kindly—was the Spanish farmer who ate his honey and saved his bees too. From the first the *Yale Walpole* has been planned as an encyclopedia of eighteenth-century life and thought. When scholars of the twenty-fifth century turn to our index I hope they will find what they are looking for.

No collector-editor can ever have been more fortunate than I have been in his associates and collaborators. The typographical honors accorded to the *Yale Walpole* were the result of Carl Rollins's devoted care and interest. Warren Smith, George Lam, and Charles Bennett have been with me many years as full-time editors in "the Walpole Factory" in the Yale Library; Grover Cronin has been with us on leave from Fordham for four years. Dayle Wallace and Allen Hazen join us in the summer, the latter at Farmington doing his bibliographies of Strawberry Hill and Walpole and the catalogue of Walpole's Library. Many Yale undergraduates have helped with the humble tasks of typing and calendaring the eighteenth-century letters, other than those to or from Walpole, in my collection. My secretary, Miss Julia McCarthy, has performed miracles of discovery in the contents of Strawberry Hill.

Because of all these people (we are now sixteen) the *Yale Walpole* has become an actuality. As a result of it scholars have been generally led to take a more serious view of Horace Walpole and his place in the literature and history of the eighteenth century. Literary and historical reputations, as Mr. Desmond MacCarthy has said, rise and fall on crests and troughs through the generations. When Walpole again descends into the critical trough, I think that the *Yale Walpole* will float along to the next crest and will remind posterity that Horace Walpole is indispensable to an understanding of his time. "Nothing gives so just an idea of an age as genuine letters," he wrote; "nay, history waits for its last seal from them." The history of the eighteenth century bears the Walpolian seal.

This is not the place to discuss the complicated editorial questions that faced me in 1933 when I began the *Yale Walpole*: Should the letters be edited chronologically from the first letter Walpole wrote in his eighth year to the last letter he wrote in his eightieth—or by individual correspondences? Should the letters be printed exactly as they were written with all their eccentricities of spelling, punctuation, and capitalization or "normalized"? (A question that sharply divides the scholarly world.) The mysteries and enchantments of indexing could alone fill a long chapter. It is tempting to dwell on the subtleties of *ibid., idem, op. cit., loc. cit.,* and that firefly of the scholarly swamps, *cf.;* to set down my views on what footnotes should be and how they should be written and presented on the page; to raise questions of method and style; to describe the mechanics of the *Yale Walpole;* but all that would make another book. Here we are primarily concerned with collecting and my first and continuing job. That was and is to find the originals of all the letters to and from Walpole in existence.

XII

I

AT A guess, there are some 4,000 Walpole letters in existence and some 3,000 letters to him. In 1933, thanks to the prefaces of the Toynbees, I knew that Lord Waldegrave had about 900 Walpole letters, the Duke of Manchester about 450, the British Museum and the Morgan Library about 200 each. I had something over 100 in my own collection and knew of smaller collections here and there. Where were the missing 5,000?

The greatest sleuth of letters between the wars was Seymour de Ricci, whose generosity about Bentley's drawings seven years before I had not forgotten. By means of his catalogues, his filing system, and his memory he performed miracles of discovery. If anyone could tell me where letters to and from Walpole were, it was he. So, as soon as the *Yale Walpole* was started in 1933, my wife and I went over to Paris to consult him.

De Ricci was a tall man, a rather alarming man, a melting-pot of learning and races, French, English,

Italian, Jewish. He had studied under the greatest scholars of Europe and written a dozen books that are landmarks in bibliography. There was something commanding and unearthly about him. I would not have been surprised if he had vanished before my eyes, leaving behind a faint smell of sulphur.

His flat was on the ground floor in the rue Boissière. Only a ground floor could support the weight of his thirty thousand auction-sale catalogues. Mme de Ricci came in while I was telling her husband of my problem. We stood in the drawing-room, which had sale catalogues from floor to ceiling, on the tables, chairs, and floor. "Books!" she cried with loathing. "Would you like to see where I hang my dresses?" I followed her into her bedroom, where she threw open the closet door. There, leaving no space for a single dress, were rows and rows of auction-sale catalogues. "Books everywhere!" she said with hatred and despair, and abruptly left us.

I had two questions for de Ricci of immediate concern to me: Where were Mme du Deffand's and Cole's letters to Walpole? I asked about Mme du Deffand's first. He answered at once. "They were sold in the Strawberry Hill Sale, April 1842, lot 107, to a Eurasian named Dyce Sombre, of Meaford Hall, Stone, Staffs. They were resold in the Parker-Jervis Sale at Sotheby's, 12 March 1920, lot 387, to a book-

seller for Paget Toynbee, who gave them to the Bodleian, where they now are." De Ricci gazed at me; no
doubt he was thinking, as was I, that I really should
have known all that myself.

Cole's letters to Walpole were more of a problem.
They had been sold at the Strawberry Hill Sale to
Henry Colburn, the publisher. So much I told de
Ricci, who went on rapidly from there: Colburn's
partner was Richard Bentley, who in the middle of
the nineteenth century brought out many eighteenth-
century memoirs and collections of letters. I should
write to his grandson, Richard Bentley, who was living at The Mere, Upton, Slough, and who was re-
puted to have vast collections of manuscripts inherited from the great days of his family's firm. This,
as I shall presently relate, I fortunately did.

For a week de Ricci instructed me in the mysteries
of finding letters and other objects and the art of
cataloguing them when found. He put aside the
proofs of his *Census of Western Manuscripts in the
United States*, to the justified annoyance of the American Council of Learned Societies, which was bringing out the work, in order to concentrate upon my
problem. The secret of success, he said, was a thor-
ough search of auction-sales catalogues and records.
This was the first thing to do. "My methods," he said,
"have added ten per cent to the canon of Shelley

letters, and Shelley letters have been much more collected than Walpole's." It was as if he had summoned
them from the vasty deep. He forthwith put one of
his assistants to work searching his catalogues for me
at a nominal fee. Later in the summer he followed
my wife and me to London, where he spent many
days in the British Museum going through the catalogues that he did not have in his own collection. De
Ricci's contributions were so dazzling that it was
sixteen years before I realized that his history of Walpole's letters was far from complete. Then the catalogues in the British Museum and New York were
thoroughly searched. As a result of this mopping-up,
records of hundreds of "new" letters were found and
the extracts from them as printed in the catalogues
were recovered. The advice that de Ricci gave me
about cataloguing and filing letters has proved to be
excellent. I am sorry that I did not follow all of it.
The only reason I didn't, I think, was an unwilling-
ness to play Trilby to his Svengali.

2

There are other ways of looking for letters. The
first that a new editor of an Englishman's letters usually tries is to send a letter to the *Times Literary
Supplement* of London. The new editor announces
his project and requests the loan of such letters as its

readers may have. He asks permission to copy them and promises to return them promptly. Then he sits back and waits for the letters to pour in on him. I did this a few years earlier when I thought of editing the letters to George Selwyn. My letter brought one reply. It was from a man who had written a book on Selwyn; he assured me that he had exhausted the subject and that there was no use in my trying to find other unpublished letters to Selwyn. (I now have nearly three hundred.) After the *Yale Walpole* was launched I did write to the *TLS* by way of announcing it. Although the editors kindly gave my letter the place of honor in their Correspondents' Column, I got no reply to it, nor did I expect one. The editor's journey is not often shortened by any such cross-cut.

Another source of discovery, I was told, is Somerset House, the place where English wills are kept. This sounds logical. You begin with the will of the person who received the letters you are after and then proceed through generation after generation until you find the letters in a country house in Shropshire. I engaged a professional searcher of wills in an effort to find the letters that Walpole wrote to his sister, Lady Mary Churchill. Theirs must have been an immense correspondence, since Walpole and his sister wrote to each other frequently for fifty years. By the terms of Walpole's will his letters were returned to the correspondents who survived him. Lady Mary outlived him and so must have got back all her letters to him when he died. Not one letter that passed between them has ever been printed. If the letters still exist, they are probably all together in one place. Where is this place? I asked.

Lady Mary had a large family, all of whom were equally fruitful. Her progeny became an army that followed the flag around the earth. Grandchildren went to India; great-grandchildren to New Zealand; heaven knows where the great-great-grandchildren got to, for I gave up when we came to them. Then, quite by accident, I met one of Lady Mary's descendants, a lady who knew all about the letters. I recognized the lady's name as one of the names that had been churned up at Somerset House. It seemed too good to be true. "Oh, yes," she said, "I know all about Horace Walpole's letters to Lady Mary Churchill. They belonged to my Uncle George in Dorset."

"And your Uncle George?" I asked.

"My Uncle George," she continued, "went mad one day and, screaming with laughter, threw all the letters, one by one, into the fire."

This is the nearest I've ever come to finding Walpole's letters through Somerset House.

3

There are three chief repositories of letters: bookshops, libraries, and private owners, in the order of their accessibility.

When we began the *Yale Walpole*, I had bought, as I have said, about one hundred letters in London and New York shops. Booksellers can be of great help to the collector by keeping an eye out for "his" author, by reporting anything they find, and by giving him information they usually keep to themselves. The more costly an author's letters are, the easier they are to discover in a bookshop, since only a few dealers will have them. If the new editor is able to buy them he will run the market up against himself. (He will be well-advised to accept this unpleasantness gracefully without clucking and squawking.) By giving all his bids at auctions to one dealer and letting it be known that he has done so, he will control this inflation somewhat. I gave my bids to Maggs in London and Byrne Hackett in New York. When the trade sees either of these firms bidding on a Walpole item, they know that it is probably for me and they do not usually compete for it unless they have a bid from one of their own customers.

The specialist has a great advantage over booksellers who deal in the manuscripts of many persons.

I was once shown some verses of Thomas Gray in a famous shop. They were written on the margins and back of a quarto sheet on the front of which were verses in another hand. These second verses the bookseller waved aside as of no interest. He had had the manuscript for years, he said; it was marked too high; would I care to have it at a third of the price? I would, with the swiftness that non-collectors call predatory. The price was, in my opinion, still high for the Gray, but not in conjunction with the verses that were of "no interest," since they were in the youthful hand of Horace Walpole, as of course I then said. Such experiences are dividends paid to specialists, who will also receive negative dividends by avoiding manuscripts that are "wrong." The most honorable and careful of booksellers may attribute a manuscript to an author by mistake, for there is a family resemblance in handwriting of a single generation, and handwriting experts are few.

Closely allied with the booksellers are the auctioneers whose sales are a chief source of supply to the trade. When a collector becomes identified with a particular author, the auctioneers will let him know when they have received a unique item for sale before it appears in a catalogue. The partners of Sotheby's, J. E. Hodgson, and Arthur Swann of the Parke-Bernet Galleries in New York have taken this trouble

Anne Duchess of Grafton, cut at Geneva by Monsieur Hubert 1762.

SILHOUETTE OF THE DUCHESS OF GRAFTON

for me many times. Mr. Swann once did something for me that cannot have been done often in the auction business. He called my attention to several silhouettes that Walpole owned and annotated and that were to be sold at the Parke-Bernet in a few weeks' time. One of the silhouettes was of Voltaire, another was of Walpole's friend and correspondent, the Duchess of Grafton. But what was far more important to me was a list of names that Walpole had written on a slip of paper that was framed with the silhouettes. The names were notes for a missing letter to Mme du Deffand. Since only seven out of 850-odd letters of Walpole to her have survived intact, these notes were of more than usual interest. We were about to publish our du Deffand volumes. If we had to wait until the sale was held, it would be too late to include the list of names where they belonged in our edition, even assuming that I bought the lot. Mr. Swann allowed me to print the names. He had reason, of course, to believe that I would buy the lot (which I did), and that he was therefore quite safe in letting me have it, but in doing so he permitted friendliness to overcome stark legality.

As I have said, bookshops are the most accessible of the three chief repositories of letters; libraries are the second. I had an uneasy feeling that there were Walpole letters in libraries all over the world, and so, with Mr. Keogh's help, I wrote a circular letter to eight hundred of them asking for photostats to be made at my expense of any letters to or from Walpole in their collections. The results were meager: a short unpublished note in the Public Library at Melbourne, and a receipt for money received by Walpole from the Exchequer in the Prussian State Library, Berlin. Six other librarians replied that they had nothing: that is, I received eight replies to eight hundred inquiries. It may seem surprising that librarians will not respond willingly to a circular letter, that they require something more personal; but the librarian is a busy, hard-pressed man with much responsibility. Circular letters asking him for his help are rather irritating: they are too easy; let the seeker come and show that he will make good use of what he is given. Once the librarian's interest has been engaged, he can be of immense help—he and his staff—in unearthing new material.

All libraries, great and small, misplace items in their collections. Other items assume an incognito that may leave them disguised indefinitely. The "Theatre of Geo. 3" furnishes examples of the second disguise: there are still over a hundred of the plays incognito on library shelves. In a vast library like the British Museum one can imagine how many such items there must be. The discovery of the Walpoliana among them has been carried on for me there by Mr. A. J. Watson, Senior Clerk of the Department of Manuscripts. For twenty years and more he has borne Walpole in mind throughout his day, looking up our many queries and, over and over again, spotting odds and ends of Walpoliana that had escaped the museum cataloguers. His colleague, Mr. A. W. Aspital, has done the same in the Print Room. It can be imagined what it has meant to me to know that at the British Museum there have been friends tirelessly on the lookout for missing material of importance to us.

The helpfulness and courtesy of the Museum's Department of Manuscripts began at its entrance with the two guards, Maxwell and Keenan. Maxwell had been wounded during the siege of Mafeking, Keenan at Gallipoli. Maxwell was the more outgoing of the pair. His greeting lighted up the murk of Bloomsbury. If by any chance Mr. Flower or Mr. Millar was busy when I arrived, Maxwell escorted me into the glass box where the visitors waited, as if it were the royal coach. He was a perfect host, solicitous, affable, informative. Keenan, a preoccupied man, seldom spoke and never smiled. One day when I was in the box, Maxwell confided to me that Keenan had a silver plate on the top of his head as a result of Gallipoli. "He is very proud of it, sir," Maxwell said, "and he don't let everybody touch it." I sensed that

I was being prepared for a marked distinction. The last time I saw Keenan he spoke to me for the first time. Removing his cap, he said: "You may press the top of my head, sir," and bowed before me. I pressed the top of his head, gingerly. The silver plate gave slightly. Maxwell beamed. I had received the accolade.

In England librarians may join with auctioneers and booksellers in helping the collector-editor in a way that falls outside their usual course of business. This is when they are called in by the government for purposes of probate. My friends among the librarians, auctioneers, and booksellers have kept me in mind on these occasions, and when they found unique Walpoliana they have told the executors of the estate about the *Yale Walpole* and my eagerness to buy anything that would help it. My friends' sole emolument has been the satisfaction of furthering an undertaking they have believed in. Their interest has meant that I have had friends watching for me at the collectors' source, the English country house. Ours has been an Anglo-American enterprise quietly and pleasantly conducted.

4

We come now to the third set of owners, who are by all odds the most inaccessible, the private owners.

How is one to discover them and secure their co-operation?

Private owners may be divided into two groups: those who have bought their letters and those who have inherited them. Collectors of autographs are the bane of the editor. As a rule, they are content with one or two letters, to find which may cause the editor as much trouble as to find an entire correspondence. Since nearly all auction sales are to the trade, the name of the ultimate purchaser cannot often be obtained from the names printed in the records of the sales. Booksellers are reluctant to disclose the identity of their clients, but if they like the applicant they will write to the owner for permission to do so, with varying results. Many autograph-collectors have a fellow-feeling for a collector editor and may even go so far as to write him voluntarily about the letters of his man in their collection (Dr. Frank R. Pleadwell, U.S.N., Retired, of Honolulu, is a notable example of this generosity), but there are a few collectors who, henlike, having pounced on a desired leaf, race off to a corner of the hen-yard and pick at it in private.

There remains the last set of owners, the private owners, who often do not know that they own the letters. Death may be the ultimate guide to them, by bringing in the agents of the government, who go through the house with a fine-tooth comb, but the collector-editor cannot leave it all to his grisly colleague.

When I am asked how one reaches these remote and mysterious people, I am tempted to suggest a study of Henry James's *Aspern Papers*, even though that quest ended in failure. One should note that the unnamed hunter had knowledge of his subject, courage, patience (although not quite enough of it) , and a little extra money. He had good manners, *savoir-faire;* and he was an American abroad, which was a great advantage. Above all, he had a consuming passion for his author. Without that the seeker is a mere drudge. The suspense and emotions of the *Aspern Papers* do exist; they furnish the collector-editor with his best stories; but before the locked chest is opened, before the moat of the castle is crossed, hours and months must have been spent in preparation for the climax, and when the chest is opened it may be found empty, or, more bitter still, its sought-for contents may have been reduced to a heap of waste by rats and damp.

It is a strange sort of expedition that seeks to recover in a distant corner of a house the letters placed there years ago, in an hour of clearing-out and puting-away, by a person long since dead. It is a form of hide-and-seek with the past. The one who hid the treasure—most likely a woman—sat with the letters in her lap. What to do with them? Are they worth keeping? Should she burn them? She destroys some of the best—"They were much too personal"—and decides to keep the rest; they may be of interest one day to somebody, and so far as she can see, there is no harm in them. But where should she put them? The room at the end of the passage on the third floor? The cupboard in the garden house? She chooses a remote hiding-place, and years later posterity stumbles along in search of them, poking about here and there, getting hot and dirty and tired, and eventually finding what was put away, finding it this morning or tomorrow afternoon or twenty years from yesterday, at last finding what was lost; and perhaps what is found will change the lives of two young people in Nebraska or North Carolina.

XIII

I

IN LONDON in 1933 I finally followed de Ricci's suggestion that I write to Mr. Richard Bentley of The Mere, Upton, Slough, to inquire about Cole's letters to Walpole. He wrote back that he did not have them and knew nothing about them. Such a reply is a formula much used by owners to put off inquirers, but Mr. Bentley showed his goodwill by calling on my wife and me at Brown's Hotel and asking us down to Slough for lunch. We were out when he called, the date of our sailing for home was nearing, and we felt that we could not take a day off for a visit that promised nothing in the way of missing letters.

Meanwhile, my associate Dayle Wallace, working in the Yale Library, discovered the whereabouts of Cole's letters to Walpole from the catalogue of the Forster Collection in the Victoria and Albert Museum. The letters had got there by a short route: Colburn left them to his widow, who married Forster, who gave them to the museum. The search for manuscripts *may* be done quietly at home.

And there my connection with Mr. Bentley and The Mere, Upton, Slough, might have ended if I hadn't one day during the following winter glanced into a book I seldom opened, and read by chance a footnote that answered another question I had been asking. The question was: where are the letters of Horace Mann to Walpole? He and Walpole corresponded for forty-five years without a meeting, from 1741, when Walpole's visit to Florence ended, until 1786, when Mann died. This correspondence consists of over seventeen hundred letters, many of them of great length. If all of Walpole's other letters had been destroyed, his letters to Mann would have brought him lasting reputation. Mann's letters to Walpole had been published in part by Bentley in 1876 in an unsatisfactory book called *Mann and Manners in Florence*. I knew that Walpole's letters to Mann belonged to Lord Waldegrave, but where were Mann's letters to Walpole? The answer to my question was furnished by the footnote: they were in the possession of Mr. Richard Bentley, The Mere, Upton, Slough, Bucks. My original letter to Mr. Bentley had asked only about Cole's letters to Walpole. Before volunteering further information Mr. Bentley had, naturally, wished to have a look at the inquirer. Failing to meet him, he returned to Slough and said nothing about Mann's letters to Walpole.

The discovery that Mr. Bentley owned them, all 877 of them, awakened our correspondence. It proceeded cautiously at first; on Mr. Bentley's side it might be said to have yawned and stretched. A postcard that I sent him from California that summer stimulated it; a postcard of a palm tree, it was. (The pulse of any Englishman is quickened by the sight of a palm tree.) I assumed that he would not care to part with Mann's letters, but could I have them photostated? He was troubled by the expense which that course would put me to; he came more and more to believe that I should have the letters themselves. They arrived at Farmington in time for Christmas for a sum considerably less than the cost of photostating them would have been.

Six months were to pass before we met, but in the interval our correspondence rose to the regularity and fullness of Mann's and Walpole's. They had been concerned with the rise and fall of ministries and the marching and countermarching of armies across Europe; Mr. Bentley and I were concerned with the minutiæ of editing. We were merely Walpole's trainbearers, but trainbearing is an office that ensures its holders a good view of what is taking place.

Mr. Bentley's epistolary style was enlivened by the use of block letters and red ink. He darted off into delightful bypaths from the main highway of our subject—bypaths that might lead to the **Duke of Wellington** or Henry VII's Queen. A stream of books and pamphlets of his authorship began arriving, including *A brief Note upon the Battle of Sainte and Mauron, 1351 and 1352*; and *Upwards of Sixty Years' Rainfall at Upton, Slough, Buckinghamshire, including hail, sleet, snow, hoar frost or mist*. Our acquaintance was well advanced when my wife and I made our next annual visit to England and he wrote to Brown's:

"The 12:15 from Paddington on Tuesday next [in red ink]. Excellent. You should discover on the platform at Slough an octogenarian with white whiskers (and a projecting white moustache) looking out as passengers descend from the train—on the lookout for you."

This visit had a double mission. I wanted to meet Mr. Bentley and thank him in person for letting me have Mann's letters, and I wanted to see if he had other Walpole manuscripts. I had learned one of the axioms of collecting: where there is one good thing, there will be others.

Specifically I had in mind Walpole's correspondence with William Mason, the poet and biographer of Gray. The Bentley firm had published it in 1851, since when the originals had not been seen by any subsequent editor. This suggested that one or both sides of it might still be at Upton. That is, this second mission was an Aspern Papers mission.

There was at Upton, so Michael Sadleir told me, a book in which was recorded a brief history of each of the Bentley publications. Mr. Bentley was loath to show this book; but he would, if pressed, one might almost say cornered, remove it from its hiding-place, answer the specific question asked, and put it away again. The success of the second of my two missions depended upon my discovering what that book had to say about the Walpole-Mason correspondence.

2

There was no mistaking Mr. Bentley, even without the identifying whiskers. The stout, short, figure in a bright checked waistcoat and a square bowler hat could be no other. We got into a massive automobile and rolled away to Upton, to a large "black and white" house built in the 1890's and set in ample grounds.

In the hall was a grandfather's clock with a notice: "True Time—False Time is one hour in advance." My wife and I were led into a large room on the left. At a long table in the center was a lifelike Negro boy in iron, dressed as a jockey. It was so lifelike that in the rather dim light we were startled. Mr. Bentley was enchanted.

"What do you think he once did?" he asked. We couldn't imagine. "Blew up!" said Mr. Bentley, "when a parlormaid moved him too near the fire." He had been so skillfully mended that, as we could see for ourselves, there was hardly a trace of the accident. We were not told of the repairs to the parlormaid.

At the end of the table were sherry and biscuits. We sat ceremoniously, and Mr. Bentley launched forth upon the story of Queen Victoria's wedding. He dropped into dialogue at the climax when the organ refused to work, and acted out the consternation of Sir Somebody Something, who was responsible for the failure. During this narration a lady entered the room and hurried around to sit beside Mr. Bentley. Since the English are casual about introductions, it was some time before we discovered that she was Mrs. Bentley.

It was clear that our host was in no hurry to reach the subject of Walpole, and, that being so, importunity was to be avoided. Nothing could be less like the Venetian palace where the Aspern Papers were housed than The Mere, but in it on that day there was the same expectancy and something of the same reticence in gratifying it.

An opening occurred when we went into the neighboring drawing-room, for on its walls were several copies of miniatures formerly at Strawberry Hill. Not to notice or comment on them would have been quixotic. The comment having been made and no ill effects being evident, I went on to observe that often owners of books and manuscripts and objects of art did not know that they owned them. "There might be, for example," I said, "letters of Walpole right here in this house." Mr. Bentley's steady stare suggested that I had perhaps been precipitate, and I did not bring up the Walpole-Mason correspondence until at lunch, when a second opening offered itself.

This time, greatly daring, I came right out in the open. "The Walpole-Mason letters were published by Bentley's," I said. "Could they be here?"

"I have a book," said Mr. Bentley, brushing the subject away as if it were a crumb, "which will answer that question."

We were interrupted by a message from the gardener. An earlier message had read: "Upton, Slough, Bucks, July 16, 1935, 2:05, True Time. 79 ½° F."

"You see," Mr. Bentley had said, "it's almost 80!"

A second message reported that the thermometer had crossed 80, and congratulations went round the table. A *very* hot day!

With the disappearance of the strawberries I ventured to ask our host: "And now the book?"

He looked at me stonily. "You must see the house first."

We wandered through the bedrooms and settled in an upstairs sitting-room. Mr. Bentley opened a cabinet filled with curiosities. He gave my wife a purse. "Money, it is said, is the root of all evil; yet we can't do without money, and a purse is as convenient a way to carry it as any other. Now, madam, look inside that purse." She opened it and out flew a spring.

After more surprises of a similar nature, we left the room. Mr. Bentley anticipated my question. "But you haven't seen Windsor!" he cried. We climbed up into a cupola from which we could see Windsor through the trees, Mr. Bentley prudently remaining below. As we came down the stairs, he pointed to the wall and began rapidly: "You would say, Mr. Lewis, that this is the end of the house?"

"I would."

"Let us see." He pressed a button, a door slid back, and there was another wing of the house fitted up as a ship: port and starboard lights, oars, staterooms, life preservers. A dumb-waiter that led to the kitchen —or galley when approached from this quarter—received orders that began with "Ahoy!"

"Now," said Mr. Bentley, "the book!" and he gave me a crafty look.

We went back to the dining-room, where the book had been the whole time during lunch. He took it and sat on the arm of a large stuffed chair.

"What year were the Mason letters published?"

"1851."

He struggled with the book, which was hard to handle sitting in that position. "Here, you take it," he said.

I turned to "The Correspondence of Horace Walpole, Earl of Orford, and the Rev. William Mason. Now first published from the original MSS. Edited, with notes, by the Rev. J. Mitford. In Two Volumes. London: Richard Bentley, Publishers in Ordinary to Her Majesty. 1851." I came to the end of the page and read: "The originals of Mason's letters to Walpole are now [1900] in the possession of Mr. Richard Bentley of Upton, Slough, Bucks." As I read this last aloud, Mr. Bentley fell over into the chair, his short legs sticking above the arm. He was breathing heavily. "What a very pertinacious young man!" I heard him say.

"Have you given the letters away?" I asked.

"No."

"Have you sold them?"

"No."

"Then they must still be here!"

There was a pause. "Time for tea," said Mr. Bentley firmly, struggling up out of the chair and taking the book from me.

Letters sped back and forth from Upton to Brown's. On the 18th, in answer to my letter written on our return after tea, came this one:

"Six possible fields of research are open. (Four libraries in the House itself, one one hundred yards away easterly and one one hundred yards distant— north westerly. Total six. . . ."

Five days later he wrote: "The chase goes on—at intervals—between inrushes of visitors—because I feel that you are RIGHT, i.e., if the books have *not* left Upton (which I am sure is the case) —they must be here still [in red]."

Another letter arrived on the 28th. Libraries one to six had drawn blank, but a friend had seen Mason "somewhere upstairs." "Now the search light has to be turned at every free interval upon subsidiary or supplemental collections—and *now* with a certainty of ultimate success."

That week-end we spent in Norfolk, and on our return I wrote to Mr. Bentley (in the clairvoyant style his correspondents acquired) that as we approached Liverpool Street my wife and I had said to each other: "Mr. Bentley will find the letters this week."

On the following Tuesday came a "Greetings Telegram" with a gold border, and in a gold envelope with the message printed by hand: "Eureka! Mason. Bentley," which was soon followed by two letters, both written on the same day. The second was in acknowledgment of my greetings telegram to him, which reminded him, because it was so different, of the manner in which the Duke of Marlborough sent the news of Blenheim to Queen Anne. He brought the letters up to London and turned them over to me for a nominal sum a few days later.

Letters and postcards continued to arrive with excellent advice about editing and with remarkably shrewd guesses and surmises about Walpolian problems. He was a constant reader of *Notes and Queries*, in which dozens of our queries relating to the Cole correspondence had begun to appear, and he never failed to send me a reply when he had something he thought might be of interest. Then, quite suddenly, in February 1936, he died.

3

It was Robin Flower at the British Museum who first told me, on our arrival in 1937, of the cache of Walpole manuscripts that he had found at Upton when he had gone down to appraise the library for tax purposes. Piled away in a box in a remote passageway—not in libraries one to six—was a collection of

Short Notes
of the life of
Horatio Walpole
youngest Son of
Sr Robert Walpole Earl of Orford
and of
Catherine Shorter, his first Wife.

I was born in Arlington street near St James's London Sept. 24. 1717. O.S. My Godfathers were Charles Fitzroy Duke of Grafton, & my uncle Horatio Walpole; my Godmother, my aunt, Dorothy Lady Viscountess Townshend.

I was inoculated for the small pox in 1724.

In 1725 I went to Bexley in Kent with my cousins the four younger sons of Lord Townshend & with a Tutor, Edward Weston, one of the sons of Stephen Bishop of Exeter, & continued there some months. The next summer I had the same education at Twickenham, Middlesex; & the intervening winters I went every day to study under Mr Weston at Ld Townshend's. April 26. 1727. I went to Eton school, where Mr Henry Bland, (since Prebendary of Durham) eldest son of Dr Henry Bland, Master of the school, & since Provost of Eton & Dean of Durham, was my Tutor.

Lincoln's Inn v. next page.

+ I left Eton school Sept. 23. 1734: and March 11th 1735 went to King's college, Cambridge. My public Tutor was Mr John Smith; my private Mr Ansley. afterwards Mr John Whaley was my Tutor. I went to lectures in civil law to Dr Dickins of Trinity hall. to mathematical lectures to blind Professor Saunderson, for a short time: afterwards Mr Trevigar read lectures to me in mathematics & philosophy. I heard Dr Battie's anatomical lectures. I had learned French at Eton; I learned Italian at Cambridge of Signor Piazza. at home I learned to dance & fence; & to draw of Bernard Lens, master to the Duke & Princesses.

FIRST PAGE OF WALPOLE'S "SHORT NOTES"

letters and manuscripts that correspond roughly in importance to that part of the Boswell cache that turned up in the croquet box at Malahide Castle. There were one hundred letters to and from Walpole, all unpublished, and a large collection of manuscripts —the manuscript of Walpole's *Short Notes of My Life* (the most important Walpole manuscript extant, I think); his first unpublished attempt at writing history, *The War with Spain* (1739); his last unpublished *Memoirs; Hieroglyphic Tales,* with two unpublished tales; essays, verses, and a mass of notes for his earlier *Memoirs.*

Thanks to the good offices of Mrs. Bentley and Mr. John Hodgson, her trustees let me have the lot en bloc. Even so, the Upton saga was not finished, for Mrs. Bentley kept finding Walpolian bits here and there—Peter Cunningham's letters to the first Bentley about his edition of Walpole's letters, Miss Berry's letters to him about her books. Mrs. Bentley sent these documents to me as soon as they were discovered. Apart from them and the Walpole manuscripts, there had been in all at Upton over eleven hundred letters to and from Walpole. This is nearly half of the original Walpole letters in my collection and more than one sixth of all that have been found. By being out when Mr. Bentley first called and by not immediately accepting his invitation to go down to Upton I nearly missed the richest find I have yet made and one of the most delightful chapters of my collecting life.

Walpole's letters to Mason are still undiscovered, in spite of extensive efforts to find them. Promising leads have come to nothing: some years ago hope flickered of finding them in Yorkshire; recently it glowed in Wales. I hope these letters are in existence, awaiting their appointed hour to re-emerge into the light. It would be pleasant if that moment struck as a result of their owner's reading this page.

4

Our friendship with the Wallers was also due to a sale catalogue.

When Walpole died, his manuscripts and letters were divided among three people, one of whom was his cousin Ann Seymour Damer, the sculptress. Her portion contained the "Journal of the Printing Office," which is Walpole's record of the Strawberry Hill Press; three "Books of Materials," which have Horace Walpole's random notes of nearly forty years —"Such scraps," he called them, quoting Cibber, "as may not perhaps be worth the reader's notice; but if they are such as tempt me to write them, why may not I hope that in this wide world there may be many an idle soul no wiser than myself, who may be equally

tempted to read them?"—his Book of Visitors to
Strawberry Hill; the Journals of his five trips to
Paris; and a large collection of odds and ends. In addition to these manuscripts were 77 letters from Walpole, of which 58 were "new," and 310 letters to him,
all "new" except 108 letters from Thomas Gray.

On Mrs. Damer's death in 1828, she left her collection of Walpole's papers to a Twickenham neighbor,
Sir Wathen Waller, Bt., in whose family they remained for nearly a century. Shortly before 1914 the
then owner, Sir Francis Waller, allowed Paget Toynbee to edit the letters. The collection was sold by Sir
Francis's brother, Sir Wathen, at Sotheby's in December 1921, just three years before I began collecting
Walpole. There were 198 lots in the sale, which was
the largest and most important public sale of Walpole
manuscripts ever held. About thirty persons appear
as the purchasers at it, nearly all of them booksellers
who resold the other manuscripts, but who were stuck
with most of the letters.

A sale of manuscripts is like the wind that rushed
into the Sibyl's cave and blew the leaves to the four
corners of the world. I began finding letters from the
Waller Sale far from Sotheby's: de Ricci gave me six
letters to Walpole in Paris; a few had reached New
York; four turned up in Honolulu, two in Dunedin,
New Zealand. The three "Books of Materials" and

some letters had got to the Folger Library in Washington; Mr. Percival Merritt owned the "Paris Journals" and the Book of Visitors to Strawberry Hill. I presently bought the "Journal of the Printing Office" and a few other pieces.

In 1933 I showed my priced copy of the sale catalogue with the names of the purchasers of each lot to Seymour de Ricci, who saw at once that several of the names were fictitious. The use of such names is sanctioned by British practice for lots that have been bought in by the owner. In the Waller Sale nearly two fifths of the entire sale, including Gray's letters to Walpole, had apparently been bought in and were therefore still in the possession of Sir Wathen Waller at Woodcote, Warwick. When I wrote to Sir Wathen about them he answered that he owned these letters and manuscripts, and added, although I had not asked the question, that they were not for sale.

That winter in New York, Mr. Arundell Esdaile, who was then Secretary of the British Museum, told me that he had just seen in Chicago a collection of letters to Walpole. They belonged to one Thomas Conolly, a plasterer at the Auditorium Hotel. I wrote Mr. Conolly on the letter paper of the *Yale Edition of Horace Walpole's Correspondence* with its Advisory Committee of eminent sponsors; he answered on the letter paper of the Julia Marlowe Beauty Shop, an establishment founded by his late wife, who, the heading stated, was the "Inventor of the Electro Vacu Treatment and Julia Marlowe Cream." Down the margin of Mrs. Conolly's paper were her sponsors, who included Julia Marlowe, Ellen Terry, Galli-Curci, Geraldine Farrar, William Gillette, Louise Homer, Harry Lauder, and Carmen Superba.

That summer I called on Mr. Conolly in his house, not far from the university. He was a short, stocky, man, aged (as he told me) seventy-seven, with the intense expression of the lifelong collector who wants to be certain that strangers do not think his hobby is proof of madness. His person proved, here and there, that he still followed the trade of plastering. After a considerable interval he took me into the dining-room. On the table were the letters to Walpole, fifty-four of them. They were all from persons of title, the Prince de Beauveau, Lords Cholmondeley, Cork, Dacre, Egremont, and so on through the alphabet. Later in the evening he brought out many of his other letters, a collection that included Francis I and Thackeray. Whenever he got a letter from a new man, he went to the University library and read up about him. Many of his letters were from minor eighteenth-century theater people, whom we discussed. Murphy, I recall, was more to his taste than Foote, but Conolly was a kindly man. Finally, he showed me the pride of his collection, the circus posters in the cellar.

As a young man in Yorkshire he had been an ardent member of an evangelical set. He and his closest friend took vows dedicating themselves to industry and honesty that they might enjoy the rewards of a life well spent. Shortly afterwards Conolly was recruited to go to Chicago as a plasterer in the Auditorium Hotel, which was then being built, and there he spent the rest of his life. It was a good place for a collector of autographs to be, for in those days of "the road" all the leading singers and actors in the world stopped at the Auditorium. His favorite among them was Ellen Terry, who in 1921 invited him to England for the summer.

During this visit he went to Yorkshire to see what had become of his boyhood friend of the vow. The village was surprised that Conolly had not heard that the friend was the head of one of the largest banks in Leeds. Conolly went to Leeds, but when he saw his friend's big house his courage left him and he walked away. On the following day, with better heart, he rang the bell and was welcomed by his old friend, who forthwith had him elected a Fellow of the Royal Geographical Society. At the Waller Sale that December the friend bought fifty-four letters to Walpole and gave them to Conolly.

Conolly had never parted with anything in his collection and was not disposed to do so—a well-known
Chicago collector had offended him deeply by offer-
ing to buy the whole thing—but after four years of
deliberation he decided to let me have the Walpole
letters since they would eventually go to Yale and
would meanwhile be useful for the new edition of
Walpole's correspondence. We continued to correspond, and I never went to Chicago without seeing
him. He finally developed some difficulty with his
shoulder that interfered with his plastering, a not
unwelcome affliction since it gave him more time to
arrange and study his collections. He died in his
ninetieth year, shortly after he had sent me one more
letter from the Waller Collection that had appeared,
mysteriously, in his cellar, a letter to Walpole from
the Prince and Princess de Craon, written from Florence in 1742.

After seeing Mr. Conolly's collection I wrote to
Sir Wathen Waller again, and this time he asked me
down to Woodcote for a night to look at the manuscripts and letters he had bought in. While sitting in
the railway carriage at Paddington, I realized that I
had come off without a pair of pajamas, a circumstance made the more awkward by the discovery that,
being Thursday, it was an "early closing day" at
Leamington. Fortunately, the Waller chauffeur was

a man of resource and knew how to knock on a back window of a certain draper's shop. It was a relief to think, as we swept up the drive to Woodcote, that the bootleg pajamas had completed my wardrobe.

The Wallers were waiting on the terrace with visible apprehension (Lady Waller recently confessed to me that they were braced for an elderly professor with a beard), but they were relieved by the story of the pajamas. The day was sunny, just the day for an extended tour of the gardens. After the tour and tea a servant appeared to ask me which shoes I would wear at dinner; I had put in one evening shoe and one golf shoe, both lefts. My friendship with the Wallers had begun.

After dinner the Walpoliana were spread out on the billiard table. This was a ritual repeated in the following summers when my wife and I went down for visits at Woodcote. On this first display I said nothing about the possibility of Sir Wathen's sending the manuscripts to the British Museum to be photostated, but he willingly consented to do so on my second visit. At that time we began the searches of the house that are the delight of collectors, especially when, as was always the case at Woodcote, we "found." The new manuscripts were added to the stock in the billiard-room cupboard. Our explorations on one occasion took us across the county to

Ragley, where I hoped to find Walpole's missing letters to Conway. The Wallers were as disappointed as we were when no Walpoliana came to light.

Sir Wathen died just after the war. Lady Waller sent the much-studied Walpole manuscripts to Christie's, where they were put into forty-four lots (representing seventy-eight lots of the earlier sale). I was able to get all but two of them.

Later a lacquered snuffbox that had been Walpole's arrived as a present to me from Lady Waller. During the war it had been slightly damaged by a land mine that fell near the bank where the Wallers had transferred various objects for safe-keeping, a circumstance that would have given its original owner, who spent so much time thinking of the ultimate fate of the contents of Strawberry Hill, cause for reflection.

More than two thirds of the leaves that were blown around the world in the 1921 sale have been gathered up and reassembled at Farmington. The whereabouts of most of the rest are known. Many of the remainder will turn up sooner or later, some in unexpected places. One day, for example, I opened my copy of Spence's *Polymetis*. Early in my collecting I put letters of authors in their books, a deplorable practice. A letter slid out of *Polymetis* when I opened it, a letter from Spence of October 27, 1757. The recipient's name was not on the letter, which was mostly about Richard I and might have been to any antiquary; but that it was not was revealed by Spence's closing wish: "May the press at Strawberry Hill ever flourish and abound." Missing Walpoliana may be anywhere.

XIV

I

WALPOLE'S LETTERS to Lady Ossory outnumber all others that have been printed, except those to Mann. The correspondence covers nearly forty years, during many of which Walpole wrote to her every week. They are the most highly finished letters he wrote. We feel in them, more than in any of his other correspondences, that Walpole is practicing, with the utmost care of which he was capable, the art of letter-writing.

Who was the lady that drew from him such letters for thirty-six years? Little is known of her, apart from Walpole's letters; which is strange, because during a dozen years she was a leading figure in one of the most self-conscious of societies. Until Walpole's letters to her first appeared, the reading public of the nineteenth century knew her as only one of the many eighteenth-century "beauties" who were forever on the go—dining, supping, flirting, gambling for large sums, lying-in, traveling abroad, being painted by

Reynolds and Gainsborough—until they were given over, died, and were buried at enormous expense.

Her first husband was the Duke of Grafton, who divorced her when she had a daughter by the Earl of Upper Ossory. Then she married Ossory and retired to his Bedfordshire estate. There she spent the rest of her life. Walpole sent her all the latest chit-chat, who was in, who out, who was marrying whom and how much was being settled on the young people, who were giving balls, who was dying. He amused her with accounts of the new books and plays, of Mr. Herschel's new planet, of Captain Cook's new islands, and Sir Joseph Banks's new birds and beasts. He wrote verses for her and her daughters. He overlooked nothing that might contribute to her amusement. I think Walpole was more in love with her than with any other woman. Although there was such a disparity in their ages (twenty years), his first letters to her (written in his early forties) sound a quite different note from the tone of mock gallantry that he used with Lady Mary Coke and his other lady friends. In one of these early letters it almost seems as if he were thinking of her as a successor to the Grifona, who had contributed to his education as a young man in Florence. He wrote to Lady Ossory regularly up to his final illness, the most sparkling letters that he—and perhaps any man—ever wrote.

Where, I of course asked myself when I began editing his correspondence, were the original letters that passed between them?

2

Walpole's letters to Lady Ossory were first printed in 1848, by Vernon Smith, Lord Lyveden, after which they vanished from the sight of succeeding editors. When Mrs. Toynbee was preparing her edition in 1900, she corresponded with Lord Castletown, who was then the head of the Fitzpatrick family. He was a promising lead, for Lord Ossory had been the head of that family in his day, and Lord Castletown was a nephew of Mrs. Vernon Smith. Hope of finding the long-lost letters rose when Castletown replied: "Lord Castletown has succeeded in finding out where the letters are, but as they are in Stranger's hands it may be some time before he gets them." Three years later his agent closed the correspondence with "there is some doubt if they are still in existence." Reading between the lines it was to be feared that the Stranger had put the letters into the fire, but I was bound to proceed on the assumption that he had not done so, for to edit so large and important a correspondence from a nineteenth-century text would to be put a conspicuous blemish upon our edition.

My initial attempts to find the letters ended in failure. The current Lord Lyveden, as the great-grand-son of the first editor of the letters, was the most ob-vious person to approach, but no one, not even the *Peerage*, knew where he lived. I wrote to his sister, who did not answer my letter. The *Peerage* showed several families of collaterals, and there was always Somerset House and the family wills that could be searched, but I had become skeptical of wills and col-laterals as a means of finding missing family papers.

In the summer of 1935, English friends persuaded me to advertise for letters in the "Agony Column" of the *Times*. I had understood that the "Personals" which head that column: "Come home. I love you, Alice," really mean: "It is safe to land the opium at Hull on Tuesday," and that it was not, accordingly, the place for the *Yale Walpole*, but no, I was told, everybody used the "Personals" column.

R. W. Chapman and Dudley Massey helped me with my advertisement. "HORACE WALPOLE. Mr. W. S. Lewis," it read, "Brown's Hotel, Dover Street, W.1., is anxious to secure information of the whereabouts of letters to and from Horace Walpole for use in the *Yale Edition of Horace Walpole's Cor-respondence.*" This appeared for three consecutive days, with prompt results: I was offered old laces and second-hand Rolls-Royces; two letters of a more per-sonal nature from young women offered their services to the editor in whatever capacity he might nominate; but no one mentioned Walpole except a lady in Belgrave Square who wrote to say that she had hundreds of Walpole letters, which turned out to be the printed volumes of the 1840 edition.

I was about to cross off the Agony Column as another failure when this letter arrived:

> *Bishop's Lydeard House*
> *Taunton*
>
> *August 4, 1935.*
>
> *Dear Sir, I notice an advertisement in* The Times *for correspondence of Horace Walpole. I have thirty years* [of letters] *between him and his cousin Lady Ossory—these were all published by my grandfather the Rt Honble Vernon Smith, the first Lord Lyveden: so it is possible they may be of no use to you.*
>
> *Yrs faithfully,*
> *R. Vernon.*

Lady Ossory was not Walpole's cousin, but that was a small error. I called Mr. Vernon on the telephone, an aggressive move made necessary because I was sailing soon and there was hardly time for the minuet of correspondence. Were these the originals of Walpole's letters, I asked, with the Belgrave Square lady in mind, or was he referring to the edition of them his grandfather published in 1848? These were the manuscripts, he replied; at least, they were written in ink on paper. That sounded like manuscript, all right. Might I go down that afternoon to see them? No, he was just about to leave for Cowes for a week's yachting.

"Look here," he said suddenly, "I don't know anything about you, but you are staying at Brown's, so you must be all right. I'll send them up to you."

I did not want to take the responsibility for them and, furthermore, there was the axiom: a house that has one fine thing in it will have others. It was left that my wife and I should call at Bishop's Lydeard Monday week, after lunch.

Bishop's Lydeard House is a lovely Queen Anne house protected from the road by a high brick wall. We found it in some confusion because the Vernons, fresh from Cowes, had not yet had time to put away their bags, the drawing-room was being done over, and the cook had just left. When Vernon let us in, the slight awkwardness that surrounded our meeting on this unusual introduction was not lessened by the awareness that we were wearing suits of an identical pattern.

We went into a small library on the left. "Well, there they are!" and Vernon waved at a pile of letters on the shelf.

There they were, indeed, the letters presumably

destroyed in Ireland a generation ago, one of the most brilliant collections of letters ever written. They were tied up by years in corset string, which had cut into the margins. I handled them gingerly.

"But there are not four hundred here?" I asked.

"How do you know there should be four hundred?" Vernon answered.

"I think that's the number in your grandfather's edition." He looked in the edition to see. The last letter, the famous "Pray send me no more such laurels," was numbered four hundred and two.

"Shouldn't we count them?" I asked.

Vernon got out an aged card table; we put on our spectacles and went to work. There were only about two hundred and fifty in the pile that had been awaiting us on the shelf; four more were added by Vernon when he went to have another look at the place where they had been kept. It was then that Mrs. Vernon hurried into the room, full of apologies for not being on hand when we arrived. She was, it seemed, trying to get a new cook from Taunton.

"Mr. Lewis says there should be more letters, darling. Have you any idea where they could be?"

Mrs. Vernon disappeared and returned almost at once with another batch of them, about one hundred in all. She dropped them on the table and hurried away: a cook was about to telephone. After we had counted the new lot of letters she made a third entrance.

"Dolly, dear, Mr. Lewis says there must be more still."

"Was there *ever* such a man!" She went out, immediately came back with a final batch, and left again.

I wanted to find the letters, my advertisement had said, "for use in the Yale Edition of Horace Walpole's Correspondence," as I now reminded Vernon in the interval between the final reckoning and tea. When we could, I explained, we always preferred to edit from the originals, but when we could not have the originals, photostats were a welcome substitute. It was of the greatest importance to us that we edit these miraculously recovered letters from the original manuscripts or photostats of them. Mrs. Vernon came into the room for the fifth time as I was finishing.

"You are not suggesting that you take the family papers to America?" she asked. Since that was what I was suggesting and since it was clear that the Vernons did not want to sell the letters; since, furthermore, I saw how much I was asking them to do for a stranger, I was glad to be rescued by being taken to another room, where hung a colored drawing of Lady Ossory, painted by William Hamilton for Walpole in 1773.

At tea the question of where we were spending the night came up.

"At Dunster," I replied.

"At the inn?" asked Mrs. Vernon.

"No."

"At the Castle?"

"Yes."

This changed everything, for it introduced that essential element in such affairs, a common friend, Mr. Geoffrey Luttrell, who had asked us to stay with him whenever we were in his neighborhood. I said frankly that I should like to buy the letters, but if they didn't want to sell them, couldn't I, please, have them photostated? The British Museum would do it, but many of the letters needed repairing, and I knew we did that work well at home. It was settled that they would let me have their decision in the morning.

In the morning when we called, the letters were done up in a parcel. I was to have them for a year and make what use I would of them.

3

On getting to New York I took the letters to the Public Library, where Mr. Lydenberg put all the facilities of the manuscript-repairing section at my disposal. The letters were beautifully mended, the worst-damaged being put on silk. Then the entire lot was photostated and sent to Farmington. There I discovered that forty-six of the letters were unpublished. This meant that there were probably more of Walpole's letters still at Bishop's Lydeard. They turned up the day before we got there in 1936, nearly fifty letters that had got into the attic.

The episode shows how necessary it is to expose oneself to luck. Vernon had gone up to Scotland by a day train on the first morning my advertisement appeared in the *Times*. He had only the *Times* to read, and, as one will in such circumstances, he read everything in the paper, even the personals, which he seldom looked at. "I think I'll answer this," he said to his wife. She urged him not to, but on the return journey, two days later, he noticed my third appearance in the *Times* and said: "I will write to him." Before our arrival Mrs. Vernon had prudently taken out of the chest in which they lay a generous handful of letters, as she later told us.

On Lady Ossory's death the letters had gone to her son by her first marriage, the 4th Duke of Grafton. His son, the 5th Duke, turned them over to Vernon Smith. When his son's house in Eaton Square was broken up, Robert Vernon saw the letters lying about neglected in the library and took them. In such ways may family papers come down the generations, defying all the nice calculations of will-searchers and readers of auction-sale catalogues. Perhaps some day Lady Ossory's letters to Walpole will reappear in the same casual way, but I fear they will not.

If Walpole kept Lady Ossory's letters, they went back to her on his death, according to the terms of his will, which directed that letters from living persons should be returned to them, but Vernon Smith was unable to find them when he brought out his edition in 1848. Subsequent search has failed to reveal them. The muniment room at Euston Hall (where the letters should have been) was destroyed by fire fifty years ago; whether or not the letters were there then, we must reluctantly conclude that they are no longer in existence, with one exception. One certainly escaped. Recently, while trying to identify Walpole's letters at Farmington to and from unknown correspondents, I was struck by a note in a large incisive hand. It had been in the Bentley cache. On the back of it Walpole made some notes for his *Memoirs* (he was a paper-saver) , and the letter had got among other notes by him for the *Memoirs*. There is no question who wrote the letter. It was Lady Ossory, as a comparison with a letter of hers to Selwyn proved. Walpole's use of Lady Ossory's letter as scrap paper for his *Memoirs* suggests that he did not keep her letters and that their destruction occurred more than a century before the fire at Euston.

Walpole's letters were copied by a clerk at Bentley's for £16 (Mrs. Vernon kindly gave me the Account of Publication and Sale of the book). The clerk's heart was not in his work: to overlook ten per cent of the collection was not good, even in an age of bad editing. Nine of the new Walpole letters precede any of those published, having been written while Lady Ossory was the Duchess of Grafton; thirty of the overlooked letters were written in 1778, when Walpole was at the height of his powers as a letter-writer. We read of Dr. Franklin and General Washington and the hatefulness of a war in which Englishmen fought Englishmen, but world events remain where they belong in an intimate correspondence, in the background. Of more concern to Walpole and Lady Ossory was the news brought to him one day when, as he was about to set off for Osterley Park on a party of pleasure, the postman handed him a letter from Lady Ossory in which she told him of the imminent death of Lord Ossory's sister, Lady Holland. "It more than damped all my entertainment," he replied. "It is one of those moments in which nothing is left to us but resignation and silence. . . . Life seems to me as if we were dancing on a sunny plain on the edge of a gloomy forest, when we pass in a moment from glare to gloom and darkness."

And a month later: "I have fallen into a taste that

I never had in my life, that of music. The swan, you know, Madam, is drawing towards its end, when it thinks of warbling. . . . I am quite enchanted with Mr. Gammon, the Duke of Grafton's brother-in-law. It is the most melodious voice I ever heard. . . . I was strolling in the gardens [of Hampton Court] in the evening with my nieces, who joined Lady Schaub and Lady Fitzroy, and the former asked Mr. Gammon to sing. His taste is equal to his voice, and his deep notes, the part I prefer, are calculated for the solemnity of Purcell's music, and for what I love particularly, his mad songs and the songs of sailors. It was moonlight and late, and very hot, and the lofty façade of the palace, and the trimmed yews and canal, made me fancy myself of a party in Grammont's time—so you don't wonder that by the help of imagination I never passed an evening more deliciously. When by the aid of some historic vision and local circumstance I can romance myself into pleasure, I know nothing transports me so much . . . I sometimes dream, that one day or other somebody will stroll about poor Strawberry and talk of Lady Ossory—but alas! I am no poet, and my castle is of paper, and my castle and my attachments and I, shall soon vanish and be forgotten together!"

XV

I

SALE CATALOGUES and advertising have been the most successful means of discovering Walpoliana; letters to journals and will-searching, the least. In between these two extremes are other means and devices of varying usefulness, of which magazine articles are one. The thought of reaching thousands—millions— by a magazine article is heady, but I have found it almost as illusory as the hopes raised by a letter asking for help in a weekly journal; almost, but not quite. After the chapter in this book on the library at Strawberry Hill appeared in the *Atlantic* and in the *Library* in London, four of their readers wrote to say that they had books from Walpole's library. Three of the four were strangers, and I would almost certainly not have heard of their books but for my article. Two of the books are now at Farmington; one of them (it came from a lady at Athens, Georgia) has laid in it the letter that was sent to Walpole by the man who gave him the book, a new letter and a new correspondent.

APPROACHING STRAWBERRY HILL FROM TWICKENHAM

Two other articles about the *Yale Walpole* had dramatic results.

In the summer of 1949 *The New Yorker* printed a "Profile" of me by Geoffrey Hellman. One morning two or three weeks afterwards I was reading proof on Volume XV of the *Yale Walpole*. The letter I was reading when the morning mail arrived was Walpole's letter to Samuel Lysons of February 14, 1787. This letter had not been seen by any editor of Walpole's letters since it appeared in *Bentley's Miscellany* ⟨1850⟩. In the absence of the original we had to edit the letter from the text in *Bentley's*. That text has an obvious error, in a proper name. Walpole was writing about a pack of fifteenth-century German playing cards that had recently belonged to an antiquary named Tutet. *Bentley's* printed this name Patet. Thanks to an article on the cards that had appeared in *Archæologia*, we had changed Patet to Tutet. We were certainly right in doing so, I thought on reading the proof as the morning mail arrived. In the mail was a letter from Mr. A. Conger Goodyear saying that he had read my "Profile" and thought I might like to know that he owned a Walpole letter, the letter Walpole wrote to Samuel Lysons on February 14, 1787. When the letter arrived (Mr. Goodyear gave it to me), we received the final assurance: Walpole had written Tutet.

In its October 23, 1944 number, *Life* printed a six-page article, "Life Explores World's Finest Walpole Library." When the Director of the Oriental Institute at Luxor read it, he wrote to say that Walpole's set of *Archæologia* was in their library. The reader may recall that the final elucidation of the letter I turned to when writing my paper on "Proposals for a New Edition of Horace Walpole's Correspondence" depended on seeing Walpole's set of *Archæologia* or, rather the second volume of it, in which appeared Masters's attack on Walpole's *Historic Doubts* on *Richard the Third*, since I believed that Walpole had annotated it fully in the margins. The University of Chicago, of which the Oriental Institute is a part, agreed to exchange Walpole's set of the *Archæologia* for my set of it, and after prodigious delays caused by the Egyptian authorities Walpole's set reached Farmington. Masters's "Remarks on Mr. Walpole's *Historic Doubts*" begins at page 198 of the second volume. As I hurriedly turned the pages, I saw Walpole's notes here and there, and when I reached page 198 it was clear that his pencil had been angrily employed as well on the margins of Masters's formidable attack. That was immediately and abundantly plain, as was also the fact that, by the tidying hand of one who is or will be frizzling in hell, every single one of his notes had been carefully erased. This was a variation of the quest that finds the missing papers destroyed by rats or damp.

These successes, modest as they are, compare favorably with the results of broadcasting, which, to date, has unearthed only two Walpole letters, both in Switzerland and both as a result of Wyndham Ketton-Cremer's broadcast on the Third Programme of the B.B.C. when he talked about the *Yale Walpole*. This was better than my own effort in Australia. In 1947 Melbourne University invited me to give some lectures on Walpole. Thanks to the good offices of the Vice-Chancellor, Sir John Medley, the Australian Broadcasting Company asked me to speak on their Guest of Honour Programme, which reaches about one third of the entire country. The A.B.C. proposed the subject that I most wanted to talk on, "the treasure hunt," as they called it, for letters of Horace Walpole.

After explaining who Horace Walpole was, why I was editing his letters, and why it was necessary to find as many of the originals of them as possible, I told my audience about the letter that the librarian in Melbourne, alone of all the librarians in the world, had reported, and went on to say that there might well be other letters to or from Walpole in Australia. "Perhaps," I said, "they are lying in a box at Launceston or Fremantle or Alice Springs. . . . It would be indeed remarkable if there were not letters to and from Walpole in Australia, other than the one we know about at Melbourne.

"Should anyone listening have a letter to or from him, or a book from his library, or if you know of anyone who has, I would, of course, be most grateful if you would follow the lead of the Library at Melbourne and let me know about it. There is little likelihood of Walpole's correspondence being edited again, and it is important that it be as complete as possible. The A.B.C. have very kindly consented to forward any communication sent to me on this subject. So far as I am aware, this is the first time a National broadcast has ever been made in a treasure hunt.

"I used to think how pleasant it would be if I could lean out of my London hotel window, blow on a silvery trumpet, and have all the Walpole letters in England float into the room and settle at my feet. Now, thanks to the A.B.C., I have used a more up-to-date method of announcement."

Letters floated in from all over Australia, but none, alas, were from or to Walpole. "I wish," several of the letters said, "that I had a Walpole letter; I would give it you." One correspondent wanted to give me a set of Thackeray's *Virginians* in parts, merely because Walpole is mentioned in it. This is a hundred-dollar book. Only two of the correspondents wanted to sell anything. The explanation of this friendliness and generosity is, I think, that the Australians liked the three hundred thousand Americans who took over their country during "the Occupation," that they are grateful to them for saving Australia from invasion, and that they wanted to help an American enterprise in which many people "at home" were also engaged.

The letters of two correspondents were particularly welcome. The first was from a Melbournian who had a large collection of letters from an eighteenth-century ancestor who lived in Florence. When I wrote him that I would be much interested in seeing any that mentioned Sir Horace Mann, he brought the half dozen that did mention him to my hotel. In them was the explanation of the quarrel between Mann and Walpole's nephew, the Duke of Gloucester, a puzzle that we might never have solved without those letters. Mr. Heathcote insisted upon giving them to me.

The second letter that I was particularly glad to get was from a man who enclosed a cutting from a recent Sydney auction catalogue that described a "new" Walpole letter. He did not know who had bought it or where it had gone, but when we got back to Farmington I found that it had preceded us, via Messrs. Maggs Brothers and London.

2

All collectors and scholars are indebted to what Walpole called "Serendipity." This is the faculty of making happy and accidental discoveries while looking for one thing and finding another, which is what the Princes of Serendip were continually doing in a fairy tale Walpole described to Mann. The scientific world, which owes so much to Serendipity, has revived the word and given it wide currency, particularly in connection with the discovery of penicillin. The word has also been taken up by antique dealers. My discovery of Spence's letter to Walpole while looking for a reference in Spence's *Polymetis* was Serendipity. Collectors and scholars can give many examples of this "accidental sagacity," as Walpole called it, which occurs at any place or time.

Closely akin to Serendipity is finding a desired object by accident while engaged in an activity far removed from any thought of the object discovered.

When the National Library of Peru was destroyed by fire in May 1943, a committee was formed in Washington to determine what this country should do to help. The Vice-Chairman of the committee,

Archibald MacLeish, who was then Librarian of Congress, asked me to join two others on a mission to Lima to study the situation and to advise the committee on our return. A friend asked me if I expected to find a Walpole letter in Lima, and I answered that I did.

My two companions were Keyes D. Metcalf and Lewis Hanke, Director of the Hispanic Foundation in the Library of Congress. Our mission, it was explained to us, was much more than just sending three librarians (I was one temporarily by courtesy) to Lima to report and advise on what, if anything, the United States should do about rebuilding the National Library of Peru. We inevitably became representatives of the United States, and as such our reception in Lima was a gauge by which Peru's attitude toward the United States could, at the moment, be measured. The loss of the National Library was a tragedy that could hardly be imagined by North Americans, for the library had been much more than the chief repository of books and manuscripts in Peru; it was a symbol of Peru's cultural seniority among the American republics. (Peru was conquered by the Spanish a century before the Pilgrims landed on Plymouth Rock; the University of San Marcos was founded eighty-five years before Harvard.) Our national library is not called the National Library of the United

States of America, but the Library of Congress, a title that does not inspire patriotic emotion. If the Library of Congress were destroyed, the loss to the country would be mitigated by the existence of our many other research libraries, and no one would feel that our country's cultural history had been wiped out. Peru had no such mitigation.

I happened to be the first off our plane at the Lima airport and was startled and pleased to find that we were being met by a reception committee on a red carpet. "Dr. Lewis, I presume?" asked the cultural attaché of our Embassy. "I welcome you to Peru in the name of the American Ambassador," he said, and stepped aside. I was then welcomed to Peru by five others, in the names of the President of the Republic, the National Library, the Minister of Foreign Affairs, the Office of Latin American Relations, and the Pan-agra Airways Company. We were photographed by the press, sped through the customs, and raced to our Embassy.

There were three people in Peru, we were told, upon whom the success of our mission depended. If any of them failed to extend conspicuous courtesies to us in the next few days we were advised to leave for home with all speed. The first two were the President of the Republic and the head of the extreme right-wing party. The President, Señor Manuel

Prado, received us at once with marked expressions of esteem and gratitude, which were followed in a few days by a state luncheon at the Palace. The second person whose favor was needed, Señor José de la Riva-Agüero y Osma, entertained us at luncheon at the earliest possible moment in the most conspicuous possible place, the middle of the large dining-room at the Hotel Bolivar. These attentions were gratifying, but after three full days in Lima we had received no sign of recognition from the third person, whose favorable notice we were assured was in some respects the most desirable of all. In spite of the extraordinary interest in our visit, which showed itself by stories of our comings and goings printed on the front pages of every edition of all the Lima papers, the Embassy was getting worried. The position of Mrs. Gallagher de Parks in the *mundo intelectual* of Peru was remarkable because of her wide travels and knowledge of the literatures of several countries and her support of the arts. Mrs. Jack Gardner of Boston perhaps came closer to her than any other American woman, but Mrs. Parks's influence was on a national scale and it was unchallenged.

On the fourth day of our visit, the Counselor of our Embassy gave a cocktail party for us. If Mrs. Parks did not come to it we were planning to leave Peru as soon as possible.

The Counselor was showing me his fine collection of French Impressionists in a back room when she arrived. We hurried out to meet her. Everyone was standing. Mrs. Parks advanced slowly to the center of the room, looked about, and asked: "Which is Mr. Lewis?"

I stumbled forward.

She smiled. "I have an unpublished letter of Horace Walpole," she said.

We completed our mission.

This near-Serendipity manifested itself to my wife and me in 1947 when we dined at Canberra with our Ambassador, Mr. Robert Butler, and Mrs. Butler. Over the fireplace in the dining-room was a portrait, by the little-known English eighteenth-century painter Henry Walton, of Horace Walpole, Earl of Orford, not the letter-writer, but his first cousin "Pigwiggin," whose identical name and title have caused confusion during the years. I saw a print of this portrait in the National Portrait Gallery in London in 1937, when the gallery held an "inquest" on a Hone alleged to be of Walpole. I had never believed that the Hone was a portrait of Walpole, and said so one day to Sir Henry Hake, the Director of the Gallery. At the inquest (we were a jury of three) I was able to prove that the Hone was not Horace Walpole the letter-writer, and Hake by producing a print of the

Walton proved that it was Pigwiggin. The Hone went forthwith to the cellar and the postcards of it were withdrawn from the racks. I occasionally wondered about the original Walton. Where had it got to? Although Walpole cared less than nothing for his ugly cousin, Pigwiggin does make a figure in the Walpolian history. It was pleasant finding Walton's excellent portrait of him on a eucalyptus-covered hill in Australia, and it is even pleasanter for me to see it now, owing to Mr. Butler's willingness to part with it, in the long hall at Farmington.

Serendipity leads collectors into the mysterious extra-sensory world where telepathy, clairvoyance, and premonition are commonplace. Making all allowances for the collector's tendency to dress up his discoveries and to forget the times when these occult impulses led to nothing, there remains a good deal that cannot be accounted for by the five senses.

All ardent collectors believe that they have a sixth sense when it comes to their men. I have told how I picked out a play from Strawberry Hill among thirty thousand plays, all bound in manila wrappers at the Folger Library. Several times I have had hunches to go to bookshops where I have never been before and I have always found important Walpoliana there. If when riding in a bus or taxi I see or pass a shop in which I am sure there is something for me, I will get off the bus or stop the taxi, will go into the shop, and not be disappointed.

The force (whatever it is) that Walpoliana exerts on me operates from private as well as public shelves. Roger Senhouse very kindly brought two books formerly at Strawberry Hill to show me one day in London. The following afternoon I had tea at his flat. We were sitting in a good-sized room, with books from the floor to the ceiling, perhaps three thousand in all. Across the room from me was a large piece of furniture that shut off the view of the books behind it. On the top of it were several jars. Without thinking what I was doing (if I had thought, I wouldn't have done it, for it was not very polite), I got up, walked across the room, set the jars on the floor, heaved the heavy piece of furniture away from the bookshelves, reached down behind it, and brought up a book with Walpole's bookplate in it. My host turned pale. "I've heard that you do this sort of thing," he said, "but I didn't believe it. I have been trying to find that book for three weeks, ever since I heard you were in London." Whatever the explanation is of "this sort of thing," it is extremely helpful in finding what has been lost.

3

Finally, there are friends. Three dozen of them have given me Walpole letters and books from Strawberry Hill. Friends also pass you on to their friends and acquaintances who own material you want to see, use, or possess. Such friends provide sponsorship as well as an introduction. Without friends it is often impossible for the searchers to overcome the natural reluctance of owners to reveal their possessions to strangers. I have had the benefit in the *Yale Walpole* of an Advisory Committee of English and American eighteenth-century experts who have acted as an official family of friends. They have helped me by making additions and corrections in our proofs, by keeping an eye out for unique Walpoliana, and by lending their names as sponsors of the project. The letterhead of the *Yale Walpole*, on which the Advisory Committee appears, overwhelms all barriers.

There are now eighteen members of the committee: R. W. Chapman, Sir Henry Hake, R. W. Ketton-Cremer, Eric Millar, Sir Owen Morshead, L. B. Namier, and Lord Waldegrave are the British; Leonard Bacon, A. G. Feuillerat, E. S. Furniss, Allen T. Hazen, F. W. Hilles, Andrew Keogh, Bernhard Knollenberg, Wallace Notestein, Frederick A. Pottle, C. B.

Tinker, and Thornton Wilder are the Americans. Three others, when alive, took an almost paternal interest in the undertaking; Leonard Whibley of Cambridge, Robin Flower of the British Museum, and Karl Young of Yale. These twenty-one gentlemen have spent scores of hours, in the aggregate, on the *Yale Walpole* and given me every assistance in their power.

Occasionally their help has been spectacular. There was the time when Sir Owen Morshead, the King's Librarian, volunteered to find Walpole's letters to Miss Anne Pitt. These letters were first printed in 1892. Were they still at Dropmore? If so, I of course wanted photostats of them. Morshead repaired to Dropmore, where all cabinets flew open at his approach. The search began. Everyone got very hot and dusty, but Walpole's letters to Miss Anne Pitt did not appear. The searchers reached the last cupboard. It was locked; the key to it was lost. "I am afraid we must break the lock," said Morshead. "Lewis says that the letters are here, and so they must be." The lock was broken, and there were the letters.

Much of the pleasure I have had in forming my library and in thinking about it has come from the friends and acquaintances who have helped me form it. They have written to me from Peru, Brazil, South

Africa, Australia, New Zealand, Egypt, and South Africa; from France, Germany, Italy, Switzerland, and the Netherlands; from Scotland, Ireland, Wales, and thirty-three of the forty counties of England; from eighteen states in this country, the District of Columbia, Hawaii, and Canada. Asia has yet to produce a Walpole item, but doubtless somebody will write to me from India or China in time. About the only places from which I never expect to hear of Walpoliana are Nova Zembla and the Antarctic.

Of the 7,000 letters to and from Walpole that are probably in existence, I have now found 6,000. The originals of 2,600 are at Farmington, together with 2,500 photostats; the rest have been collated with the Toynbee text. Letters among the still missing 1,000 turn up from time to time; for the past eighteen years a "new" letter has appeared at the rate of one every fortnight. I shall be disappointed (and surprised) if I do not find a large cache of "new" letters to or from Walpole in the next dozen years.

Four hundred of Walpole's letters that have been found and 2,500 of the letters to him are not in Toynbee. Records of 2,000 other letters in sale catalogues and in Walpole's correspondence have also been found, which double the number of correspondents in Toynbee. (This study of the sale catalogues has been largely the work of my associate George Lam and his assistants.) De Ricci's belief that his methods would add more than ten per cent to the Walpole canon has been justified.

LEAVING STRAWBERRY HILL

XVI

THE COLLECTOR in his progress wonders from time to time what he should do with his library "eventually." His family are probably not interested in it; they may resent and hate it if they have had to make sacrifices for it. If the collector feels that he should not burden his estate with it, two courses are open to him: he can sell it or give it to a library.

The old Anderson Galleries used to quote an extract from Edmond de Goncourt's will on the backs of their catalogues: "My wish is that my drawings, my prints, my curiosities, my books—in a word these things of art which have been the joy of my life—shall not be consigned to the cold tomb of a museum, and subjected to the stupid glance of the careless passer-by; but I require that they shall be dispersed under the hammer of the autioneer, so that the pleasure which the acquiring of each one of them has given me shall be given again, in each case, to some inheritor of my own tastes." The late Frank Hogan also directed that his library be sold, since "I do not deem it fitting that these friends of many happy hours should repose in unloved and soulless captivity. Rather, I would send them out into the world again to be the intimates of others whose loving hands and understanding hearts will fill the place left vacant by my passing."

"Restocking the stream" by selling important libraries has much to be said for it. A. E. Newton, who was a "general" collector, was of this school, and his final kindness to his friends was to make it possible for them to buy what they wanted at the auction that gave him so much pleasure to contemplate. Because of his sale I now own the two books from Walpole's library that I had long eyed unabashed at Daylesford.

There is another incentive to selling one's collection, in addition to the thought of "these friends of many hours" being clutched to understanding hearts by loving hands, and that is to secure the strange immortality of the auction room. This is to be known by a handful of people in each generation, not for any qualities of character or personality, but for ownership of articles prized by those few. To own a book formerly in the Huth, Hoe, Phillipps, or Britwell libraries is to become part of the great tradition of book-collecting. Collectors handle a book from such libraries with deference. "This book belonged to Beckford," an owner will say. "Here, you see, is a note in his hand, and there is the Hamilton Palace shelf-mark." His visitor, if he is of the initiated, will take the book reverently. He is not thinking of the splendors of Fonthill or *Vathek*, but of Beckford's library, which to him is as much a work of creation as were Beckford's house and novel. Because Beckford's library was sold at auction, bookmen will continue to buy and admire his books and will treasure the fragment of his library that has come to their shelves. If you have made a notable collection, your books will be held desirable by future bookmen. The sale catalogue of your collection will become part of bibliographical literature; you will be a collected collector; throughout eternity your name will have an honored place behind a hyphen: "This is the Mead-Heber-Utterson-MacGeorge-Blank copy," with your name in the blank.

What has the other school to offer that can compare with such fame? Not much, at a first glance, for it is true that many librarians and scholars do not handle books with loving hands and understanding hearts. Every library in the world has at some time abused its books by reckless re-binding, by trimming their edges, by perforating title-pages with a mark of ownership, by disfiguring backs with a call-number, by removing the marks of previous ownership and so blotting out the histories of particular books; in short, by mutilating the books under its charge. Nor are many scholars bookmen. The average scholar is contemptuous of bibliophily and treats a book in mint state as he would a cheap reprint, a working copy that is expendable. A friend of mine lent an uncut copy of a book in its original boards to a distinguished scholar who returned it with its back off. "Sorry," he said, "but I dropped it." My friend had paid a large premium to get the book in fine condition. When the scholar heard about it he said: "More fool he." One does not have to read the *Psychopathology of Everyday Life* to know that when a scholar drops a book that may have cost its owner more than the scholar's monthly salary check, the scholar may be unconsciously expressing his hatred of things as they are; yet to a person who is thinking of giving his collection to a library, his mind full of high thoughts about education and its professors, it is a blow to learn that few scholars will value his gift. Why hand your "beloved friends" over to people who will destroy them?

One answer is that there is today a growing regard for books in libraries, and that if you choose your library well, your books will not be destroyed. Anyone who met Mrs. Luther Livingston in the Widener Library at Harvard or Miss Emily Hall in the Yale Rare Book Room recognized as loving hands and understanding hearts as can be found in any private collection. The Houghton and Widener Libraries at Harvard, the Mason-Franklin, Speck, and Coe Rooms at Yale, the Spencer, Arents, and Berg Collections at the New York Public Library, the Huntington, Morgan, Folger, and John Carter Brown Libraries satisfy a bookman's most exacting specifications. There is nothing of the cold tomb about them.

The new science of bibliography is also gaining ground among scholars, who see in it a new means to increase their knowledge. Bibliography not only requires books, but books in condition as nearly pristine as possible. The men and women who use a rare book room or special collection can usually be counted on to treat its books and manuscripts and maps with respect. Professor F. A. Pottle wrote in the Preface to his *Literary Career of James Boswell*: "I have the greatest respect for [dealers and collectors], and I consider that the scholar of today who makes remarks about 'mere collectors' is talking nonsense. Our science of bibliography would be sadly hampered, indeed, were it not for the generous and largely disinterested service which private collectors perform by buying and putting freely at our disposal books which our public libraries cannot or will not purchase."

Whether scholars think of their benefactors or not, it is a bibliographical tragedy to break up a special library. When a collector has gone deep into a subject and brought together extensive materials for its study, each item in it gains importance in the context of the whole. When such a library is broken up it is to re-enact the futility of Penelope's web. If the collector does not have to destroy his collection it is worse than that, for Penelope had a good reason for ripping out her work. A special collection brings together materials that are essential to an understanding of the subjects to which they relate. Since each generation looks at the world through its own eyes, opinions and judgments are forever shifting. We do not look at Shakespeare as previous generations looked at him; future generations will not look at him as we do. The most important thing about collections is that they furnish the means for each generation to make its own appraisals. The collector who gives his library for the use of posterity is, I think, making the best possible disposition of his books.

I am giving my collection to the Yale Library. It doesn't bother me in the least to think that in the future many of my books will stand unopened for years on end. Counting the number of times a book is used as a criterion of its value is to reduce a research library and its purposes to absurdity; on that basis the most valuable books in it are its telephone books. Every great library has tens of thousands of books that may not be called for once in a decade. Paradoxically, it is these books that make it great. A large percentage of them have come from collectors who believe that the right books should be available to the right man when he comes along to help him with the book he is writing or the study he is making. As Professor Tinker taught me long ago, collections, scholars, publications—these are the three essential elements of the learned process, and the second two are dependent upon the first. To make a collection that stores up something of importance to society and then place it at society's disposal is to store up civilization for posterity's use.

With this opinion I will close. If this book should encourage anyone to collect seriously, it will have been worth writing, and to him or her I send my best wishes—provided, of course, that what is collected is anything under the sun except the works and possessions of Horace Walpole.

INDEX

INDEX

i

Index

INDEX

xi

A NOTE ON THE TYPE

The text of this book was set on the Linotype in a type face called Baskerville. The face is a facsimile reproduction of types cast from molds made for John Baskerville (1706–75) from his designs. The punches for the revived Linotype Baskerville were cut under the supervision of the English printer George W. Jones.

John Baskerville's original face was one of the forerunners of the type style known as "modern face" to printers—a "modern" of the period A.D. *1800.*

The book was composed, printed, and bound by The Plimpton Press, Norwood, Massachusetts.

Typographic and binding designs are by W. A. Dwiggins.